CADET T.

MEMORIAL FOUNDATION

Inspiring and Developing Young Leaders of Character

Read Tom's Story at www.CadetTom.com.

Greater love has no one than this: to lay down one's life for one's friends. —John 15:13 (NIV)

OSD salutes military personnel, veterans, and their families.

OSD is a global, chapter-based Veteran Support Ecosystem (EIN 27-3842517) providing relevant, relatable, and sustainable impact to the military community through social, professional, and service-oriented programs. Since 2010, OSD has impacted over seven hundred thousand members of the military community through these award-winning programs. Read more at https://weareosd.org/.

WARRIOR'S CODE 001

ALSO BY MARK E. GREEN
WITH ECHO MONTGOMERY GARRETT

STEP OUT, STEP UP

Lessons Learned from a Lifetime of Transitions and Military Service

From the Authors of *Step Out, Step Up*

WARRIOR'S CODE 001

7 Vital Steps to Resiliency

MARK E. GREEN
Lieutenant Colonel, United States Army (Retired)

WITH ECHO MONTGOMERY GARRETT

BOOKLOGIX®
Alpharetta, GA

This book includes information from many personal experiences of the author as well as those from other veterans from different branches of the US Military. It is published for general reference and education with the intent of inspiring hope, increasing resilience, and improving the transition to civilian life for veterans and their families. The book is sold with the understanding that neither the authors nor publisher is engaged in rendering any legal, psychological, career, or medical advice. The authors and publisher specifically disclaim any liability, loss, or risk, directly or indirectly, for events, advice, and information presented within. If you are a military service member, veteran, or family member of a veteran or military service member and know you need assistance with your mental health, please call this 24-hour number for the Veteran Crisis Line at **1-800-273-8255, or you can text a message to 838255**. Another option is a crisis line that operates independently of the military or any government agency called the Military Hotline **888-457-4838, or text MIL1 to 839863**. This hotline connects you with veterans and others familiar with the military culture.

Although the authors and publisher have prepared this manuscript with utmost care and diligence and have made every effort to ensure the accuracy and completeness of the information contained within, we assume no responsibility for errors, inaccuracies, omissions, or inconsistencies.

ISBN: 978-1-63183-384-7 - Paperback
eISBN: 978-1-63183-385-4 - ePub
eISBN: 978-1-63183-386-1 – mobi

Library of Congress Control Number: 2018908832

Printed in the United States of America 073018

∞This paper meets the requirements of ANSI/NISO Z39.48-1992 (Permanence of Paper)

Cover and jacket design: Randall Paulk

Authors' photos: Kevin Garrett

To any and all who have sacrificed so much in service in defense of country and for all of you, my military sisters and brothers, this book is dedicated to supporting you as you make your dreams a reality one step at a time.

CONTENTS

INTRODUCTION

I am a warrior and a fighter.

This book is for all of you who have struggled in life and need to reengage with themselves first and then reorient themselves for the next big fight.

If you have transitioned out of the military or are readying yourself for transition, it is essential to prepare yourself for the single most important battle you will ever fight:

THE BATTLE WITHIN.

As for me, it was unlikely that a guy who grew up the way I did would ever achieve anything at all.

Especially after not being allowed to graduate high school with my senior class, it was unlikely I would ever graduate from Officer's School, earn a master's degree, and later a degree in law.

After two brief, failed marriages in a five-year period, it was virtually impossible for me to believe that I would finally experience a fulfilling marriage that has lasted twenty-two-plus years.

Or that after experiencing homelessness, and surviving bankruptcy, I would be able to live my dream and own a home in Hawaii.

After wrecking my hip jumping off the back of a plane

while deployed in Afghanistan and needing a hip replacement at age forty-eight, it was unlikely I'd not only pass the physical to continue in the service, but complete a triathlon within a year of the injury.

And most of all, with the adversity I experienced early in life where I came from and starting out as a private, it was unlikely I would retire from the US Army as a Lieutenant Colonel.

When I was in sixth grade, a mentor planted a seed and taught me that I could be a champion, strong in mind, body, and spirit. But that seed got buried deep under all the challenges of my teen years and early adulthood. Once I joined the Army, that seed took root, grew, and with a lot of weeding, watering, pruning, and fertilizing, that tiny seed ultimately flourished. What I've learned from my many mentors is that we all have that warrior's spirit within us. It may just be dormant and waiting for the right conditions.

At different times in our lives, we have different hopes and aspirations. We all have those moments when we need to take stock and reevaluate.

Now is one of those moments.

Maybe you've lost sight of your dreams.

Maybe you've lost hope.

Maybe you feel broken physically, mentally, or spiritually—or on every level.

Maybe you've lost yourself—who you are at your core—along the way.

Maybe you've gotten so far away from who you once were that you don't even recognize yourself anymore.

The fact that you made it here to pick up this book is a start. It only takes that one moment. This is the seed that yields new life—renewing and reinvigorating by taking care of yourself and taking stock of where you've been.

Respect that your experiences are part of what got you to where you are today. Don't minimize what you've gone through. Acknowledge it and then use this book as a bridge to help you connect with your future.

My goal in sharing what I've learned from a lifetime of transitions and thirty-four years of total military service is to help you tap into and strengthen your resilience and grit. This book isn't full of practical tips to ease the transition into civilian life by helping you secure a job. The military and close to five thousand other organizations offer that. This book challenges you to **face your biggest battles—the battle in your mind and in your heart—and win**.

A warrior's spirit is about your heart. You want something that gets your heart pumping again—something that gets you excited. Only when you identify who you are and who you aspire to be, your purpose in life—your big WHY—and what gives you hope for the future can you move forward and successfully transition to your next adventure. The possibility of remarkable resilience resides within you.

When you've suffered traumas, disappointments, betrayals, and all manner of difficulties, it's easy to slip into just going through the motions. I've been in that trough myself. But that's not really living.

The truth can sit in your heart and never find its way out in the open where it belongs, but it is still the truth. We can harbor anger, resentment, blame, and frustration toward others, but God knows our hearts and always knows the truth. Learn to forgive and move forward.

I'm talking about seizing every moment and living each and every one to its fullest. To do that, you must make the conscious choice to live a life filled with adventure and possibilities.

The Warrior's Code holds the secret to leading a triumphant life, one that you can be proud of. You can't be an effective warrior without that code, your personal truth. Knowing and understanding the Warrior's Code leads to a deeper sense of self-awareness, gratitude, and resilience.

To be a warrior means that you have a code that you live by and that guides you—especially when you are challenged and find yourself in seemingly impossible situations. We were all trained to be resilient, to take care of ourselves and our equipment. There are times when we must take care of ourselves first. That is not selfish. It is essential.

In these pages, I break down step by step how you can access and apply the Warrior's Code. You'll also find the stories of other veterans from different branches of the military and different eras. There is healing in revealing and great value in learning from the experiences of others—both from their mistakes as well as their victories.

I love my military brothers and sisters and their families, and I am eternally grateful for the opportunities I've gotten thanks to the US Army.

Connecting with others is a magical thing. That sacred space of connection is where you'll unleash the superpower that resides in all of us.

That resilient warrior's spirit gives you the courage to reengage and emerge triumphant in this new stage of your life.

STEP 1

REST TO BE YOUR BEST

Anybody who has been in an active battle zone knows it's impossible to get any good, solid rest while you are there. Even in your off-hours, you are in a constant state of hypervigilance. During my nine-month deployment to Afghanistan in my role as an Inspector General, I was responsible for the southern half of the country along the red desert from the borders of Pakistan to Iran.

I was also in the middle of working toward my law degree. Getting my assignments in on time presented a big challenge given my limited off-hours and the frequent loss of connectivity. One night I was just about to hit send on an important assignment, when the warning blared alerting us to incoming enemy rockets. I followed protocols but was determined to get that assignment submitted since I had just attached it and was about to hit the send button. In transition, I reached up until I could feel my laptop keyboard and hit send before heading to the bomb shelter.

Poor connectivity also frequently interrupted the sparse Skype sessions I had with my wife, Denise, and our son Adam, then a preteen. I felt the stress building in both relationships. My lack of rest coupled with the long hours on the ground left me tired to the bone, which magnified my feeling of being disconnected from home. Then during the last month of my deployment, I aggravated an existing physical condition when I jumped off a tailgate of the back of a C-130 aircraft during combat maneuvers.

By the time I got back home from active duty to Florida where my family was, I not only had lost twenty-three pounds, I had so much pain in my right hip that I could hardly walk. The orthopedic surgeon explained that my hip had jammed so hard into the socket when I made that leap to the ground that it damaged it beyond repair.

"You need a full hip replacement," he said, adding that I'd likely never run again or compete at taekwondo.

His words stung. I was only forty-eight years old.

As an athlete with lots of energy to burn, running has always been one of my releases and taekwondo is part of who I am. Plus, my semiannual physical fitness test at Command and General Staff College was a few months away. If I couldn't pass, I would not be able to attend, which would take away my chance of promotion to Lieutenant Colonel.

I didn't have a chance to catch my breath from being away from my family for a year and from what I'd experienced in Afghanistan. My wife, Denise, who is a nurse, and I immediately went into survival mode, figuring out a plan that would give me the best shot of rehabilitating in time to take the required physical fitness test.

Surgery was grueling, and my discomfort was compounded by my fear that I'd fail to make that deadline. I had a long road ahead of me. Rest and therapy were my only hope.

I had to learn to walk again. Denise mapped out my rehab schedule, and as soon as I could stand, she had me out on the track at the local high school, walking every afternoon. She was with me every step of the way, nudging me, encouraging me, cajoling me, and making me laugh. There were many days when no laughing was going on. The pain and physical therapy I experienced were truly a challenge I was not prepared for in life.

Going from my mind telling my foot to move and nothing happening to being able to pass the alternate aerobic event seemed at first a bridge too far. One day, I got so angry that I threw the cane down I was using to walk with. Denise was right behind me telling me to pick it up and keep going. She has a way with me no one else does.

By the time my physical fitness test came, with Denise's help and my own grit, I arrived at the school and passed. Once more I felt that high that comes from achieving something that you were told you couldn't do.

The year after my hip surgery, I tackled the Command and General Staff College Triathlon. Denise had signed up for it with a friend. I was the last one to finish that day because I was the only walker on the last leg of the triathlon. I needed to prove to myself that I could go on. I was not in competition with others that day. I was in competition with my own mind, body, and spirit. Finding that drive is the secret to going forward. It is internal, not external, and only you know how to turn it on. It is a choice.

Jason Dodge

Four years active duty as an aviation operation specialist. Began basic training at Fort Benning on the one-year anniversary of 9/11 at age twenty-four. Job: "to get birds in the sky in Iraq," eleven months and nineteen days, from January to December 2005. Air National Guard 2006–2012. Now working with Emory Healthcare Veterans Program and helps post-9/11 veterans deal with their invisible wounds.

My number-one problem is rest, or self-care. Veterans struggle with self-care. We see rest as a sign of weakness. I am getting a little better. I'm always concerned about veterans and other people around me more than I am myself. When I was in Iraq, I was on seven days a week, twelve hours a day. You can't expect somebody to go from being constantly on high alert and just be able to turn it off when you come back home. It doesn't work that way. I'm still never calm. I'm hypervigilant.

In 2014, after my request for compassionate transfer to

Florida to care for my ill mother was denied, I hit the wall emotionally. I was alone in a crummy apartment in South Atlanta and took a position in Atlanta because that was the closest the Army could get me to Florida. I had plenty of time to reflect. It slowly dawned on me that I didn't know how to rest, relax, or take a break. I had been going a thousand miles per hour for so many years, it had taken its toll.

I'd been in a state of hypervigilance ever since that night I went to sleep as an eight-year-old, dreaming of playing with my dad with the new baseball he'd given me for my birthday, and woke up to life without Dad. I'd been giving my all in service to my country for more than three decades.

Night after night, I'd station myself in a chair facing the door in that dark apartment, gun close by, because I felt I was not far from danger. In the apartment, all I had was a chair, a small lamp I bought at a thrift store for three dollars, a plastic tote to put the lamp on, my TV, and a small bed. I called it the Hobo Hotel.

As soon as I had a few days off, I was on the road, making the seven-hour drive to Orlando to see my wife and son and check on my mom.

Einstein called the definition of insanity doing the same thing over and over again yet expecting different results. I'm no Einstein, but I knew I had to make some changes and fast if I wanted to get out of the deep, dark hole of depression I was in.

I had to stop pretending I was superhuman just because I was a warrior and give myself permission to take a break every once in a while. I had hit a tipping point in life, and it was no longer about achievement. It became a battle of the mind.

That was a big shift in thinking for me.

Like many of my warrior brothers and sisters, I somehow equated needing rest with being weak. To me, there are two kinds of rest: the sleep we get, and rest we can create while we are awake. I tackled this new self-assignment with the same vigor I've attacked any problem or challenge.

Tim Boone, PhD

Joined Army in 1965, went to Infantry Officer Candidate School, then Special Forces School, did a tour of Vietnam, left the service in 1976 as a Captain. Part of groundbreaking experiential leadership program at Fort Ord in Monterey, California, to help returning officers and noncommissioned officers reintegrate. Part of the team that started the army's Organizational Development Program on how units could become more effective and cope with the negativity toward troops coming back from Vietnam. Got PhD in leadership and human behavior at US International University, San Diego, Alliant International University. Retired as senior research associate at Georgia Tech and from four-year stint as president of Georgia Tech Military Affinity Group.

I can tell you that rest was important after coming back from

Vietnam. I was sent to Fort Benning as an infantry officer where our Commanding General (CG) said, "Okay, gentlemen, we've taken a six-month course and crammed it into nine months here. We want you to take time with your families and focus on resting and recreation. Just play." In combat situations, the chemistry in your brain changes. You develop the battle mind. That chemistry change does not set you up to be successful in the everyday world here. Part of hypervigilance means you have a lot of adrenaline pumping. You tend toward risky behavior, and anxiety doesn't help you make wise decisions.

What the research showed me ran counter to what I've practiced my whole life.

Turns out that **to be at our best**, we must have **rest**.

No one can thrive while operating on minimal to no sleep—including service members and veterans.

Rest plays a vital role in physical and emotional healing. Fatigue is a killer. It clouds our thinking and causes us to make mistakes. Fatigue is your enemy.

So what can you do?

Even when you are in crisis mode, find whatever **soothes you** and **gives you peace**—even for a brief respite. For example, when I was deployed in Afghanistan, I'd listen to my favorite music while in the helicopter.

Take small breaks.

Consciously make plans and take the time to rest. Value its restorative power and protect that time. Even a twenty-minute nap is beneficial.

Take your vacation time. For too many years, I often banked some of my vacation days instead of taking the time to recharge.

Jaclyn Peters

Decided on 9/11 in eighth grade to join the Marines when older. Enlisted in 2006, left in June 2014 with rank of Sergeant. Deployed in 2008 to Afghanistan with three extensions. Now working as forensic technician for the Franklin County Coroner's Office in Columbus, Ohio.

Between leaving the Marine Corps and moving to Columbus, I took six weeks off to lay out by the pool at the place I'd been paying for three years where I never got to spend time because I worked every other weekend. It gave me a nice break, so I wasn't scrambling to move.

Ironically, about the time I was coming to my own conclusions about how important rest is for all of us, the Army Surgeon General's office released its first "Health of the Force" report in December 2015. It gave a snapshot of active-duty soldier health across thirty US-based installations in 2014. The report showed lack of sleep continued to be a major issue. I was not alone in my resistance to rest.

Some highlights:

- One in twenty active-duty soldiers is prescribed sleep medications.
- Nearly one-third of soldiers get five hours of sleep or less each night, which is linked to increased risk of behavioral health disorders, illness, and musculoskeletal injuries.
- Almost 62 percent of soldiers get fewer than seven hours of sleep each night.
- Almost half of service members report a clinically significant sleep problem that results in 33 percent reporting fatigue three or four days a week.

The full report can be found at

www.armytimes.com/healthreport.

A Rand Corporation study, sponsored by the Defense Centers of Excellence for Psychological Health and Traumatic Brain Injury, surveyed nearly two thousand troops and also found that one-third of service members average five hours or less of sleep, which increases the risk of physical and mental health problems. In comparison, only 8 percent of US adults have reported getting five or fewer hours of sleep at night. Another third of survey subjects said they typically get only six hours of shuteye per night. Nearly half the sample had "clinically significant poor sleep quality."

Many experts have linked sleep deprivation to post-traumatic stress disorder (PTSD). Burning both ends of the candle over the long haul can increase your chances of developing Alzheimer's disease and other neurological disorders, according to numerous studies that have come out the last few years.

Troops' deployment history does not seem to be a factor in their sleep problems and sleep-related behaviors, according to the report, which concluded that "sleep problems, including poor sleep quality, short sleep duration, and fatigue, were prevalent regardless of deployment history. This suggests that sleep problems may be endemic to military culture and not solely the result of being deployed."

No matter who you are, the ideal amount of sleep each night is seven to nine hours. Wearing the uniform doesn't give you immunity to that requirement. Until 2010, Army guidelines suggested only half that amount—"the four-hour rule"—but the guidelines were revised due to concerns about sleep-deprived soldiers in combat making mistakes due to impaired judgment and delayed reactions. Studies show that four or five days in a row of operating on that little sleep produces the same kind of performance levels of someone who is legally drunk, according to Rand researchers.

Taking care of yourself by getting enough sleep is no longer viewed as a sign of weakness or cowardice. In fact, the Army created the Performance Triad, which emphasizes the importance of sleep along with physical fitness and proper nutrition **to boost performance and resilience.**

Even the strongest warriors find ways to renew themselves. After performing great miracles, healing the sick, raising the dead, and preaching to thousands, Jesus would regularly go off alone or with a few of his closest friends to pray and get rejuvenated for his next mission. And the scriptures say that God rested on the seventh day.

Still, I recognize that getting the necessary rest in order to be at your best is easier said than done.

I get it. That's why I'm saying we must consciously **adopt this new training just like we do any other order**.

As a veteran, you are in charge of your actions.

If you need to take time to rest, do it.

If you need to take some time off, do it.

If you need to recuperate from physical or mental trauma, put the right plan in place and move your allies into position to give you support.

Rest is mission critical. It is not an option. It's the fuel you need to rekindle your warrior's spirit.

STEP 2
RECONNECT WITH YOURSELF AND OTHERS

After you get some much-needed rest, the next step on the path to resilience is reconnecting with those you care about most. And the number-one priority must be reconnecting with yourself during that process.

That requires you to come to grips with something first. That is the fact that you must take 100 percent responsibility for where you are in your life.

It is always easier to blame someone else for our troubles or make excuses of all kinds. Declare your mind a blame-shifting-free, no-excuses zone.

I also know that it is easy to say and hard to do. But without this all-important principle applied to your life, you will find moving forward difficult to impossible. Einstein said that the definition of insanity is doing the same thing over and over and expecting a different result. Only when you are aware that you are repeating a negative pattern can you work on changing that bad habit.

We all chase success and experience failure. We find that life doesn't always turn out the way we want. No matter how much achievement you have, without the social, emotional, and spiritual aspects of your life in order, you are bound to feel like you are missing something.

As a military officer, I learned a certain way to act, a certain way to communicate, and a certain way to perform duties. But I learned by following first as an enlisted soldier. Although I achieved some success in my career, I was left with a nagging feeling that something was off. I felt detached from myself and others but had not identified it as such. In retrospect, that disconnect of which I had an inkling had led to a past littered with failed relationships.

On August 4, 2017, as part of my preparation for my retirement and transition to civilian life, I sat in a room with more than three hundred people who were on their own journeys of becoming Certified Success Principles coaches. Jack Canfield, author of *The Success Principles* and cocreator of *Chicken Soup for the Soul* with Janet Switzer, and the number-one success coach in the Americas, asked us to get up and hug those in close proximity.

I froze.

I don't know about you, but as a Lieutenant Colonel, fighter-with-an-attitude kind of guy, that was one order that I couldn't handle.

I was the only one that day who walked out of the room unable to show this kind of vulnerability to others.

I tried to shrug off the deep anxiety Jack's simple request triggered. *I'm not a hugger*, I thought. *Never have been, never will be.*

What I learned that next day changed my life forever. I had

a little help from Deborah Sandella, PhD, RN, an award-winning psychotherapist and author of *Goodbye, Hurt & Pain: 7 Simple Steps for Health, Love, and Success.*

Jack explains that your life improves if you know the combination to the lock. You see, *Warrior's Code 001* provides its own combination to vital resilience. Without the combination, you won't be able to access your warrior's spirit and your next mission.

I had always been able to achieve most of my goals despite long odds and patted myself on the back for it. But I was missing something: love, empathy, and compassion for others. It was always easier to put on a serious face, hide behind ego, and act important. Without taking action and being in a place where I could share my love for others, I realized that I would continue to miss out on a completely fulfilled life.

As long as my denial was stopping me from accessing the code, I was locked into old behaviors, including those that had been destructive to my spirit.

So I decided to be vulnerable for the fourth time in my life. The first two times did not work out. I had loved only to lose that love in my first two marriages for one reason or another. The third time turned out to be a charm when I married my wife, Denise. We've now been married for twenty-two years. The fourth was that day in August when I realized that I was being handed the final clue for the next step in the Warrior's Code.

The secret to living an abundant life filled with joy is making meaningful connections with others. You don't know how badly you need those connections until you experience it.

That beautiful connection to other people is what makes everything click into place and allows you to access the code that unlocks your spirit and opens you to loving relationship of all kinds: deeper connection with your family and friends; more appreciation of your colleagues, students, and mentors; appreciation for those who enter your life only briefly; and wonderment and gratitude for people you never meet at all but whose actions you have heard or read about or witnessed. A critical point is that you should never forget it is okay to start again at building new relationships. When one door closes, another always opens in time, and you must trust that this lesson has proven true every time. Be patient with yourself and the process.

I still have so much more to learn in life when it comes to transition and resilience, but if I had to name one step that will propel you forward faster than the others, this is it: **Reconnect**.

Without looking at someone from a place of compassion, love, and generosity for who they are and what they are about and making them feel wanted, supported, and loved, you not only get lost in yourself, you risk losing them.

The failure to embrace this step—pouring your heart and effort into reconnecting—is at the root of why there is so much divorce, anger, alienation, and emptiness, especially among veterans and military personnel. It may be that you are choking on ego and are not willing to let go. That was me, too. Learning and growth come from getting outside our comfort zone, not staying in it.

There is a gift in everything if you look closely enough. It may not look pretty on the outside. It may not feel like a gift in the moment if you are the one dealing with it. Perhaps you are dealing with disease or physical or mental health challenges, but **loving ourselves first and then learning to fully love others** is a crucial piece of the Warrior's Code.

When I had to have my hip replaced and learn how to walk again after an injury in Afghanistan, it made me appreciate the simple things in life. I developed gratitude for the ability to take a deep breath and feel the air entering my lungs and for just being alive. It deepened my appreciation for my wife, Denise, who helped me keep fighting through my rehab on the days I wanted to quit.

We take so many things for granted in our lives when all our needs are met. We're less likely to do that when we are in the midst of struggle.

The Code is a process that allows us to experience growth as we radically change our mindset.

To become a resilient warrior who adopts the Code, you must fully embrace the concept of loving yourself and others. Without the second half of that—loving others—you're missing one of the key steps.

A second area of reconnecting is being able to readjust. Do you ever feel like you're on autopilot, just going through the motions? You may be out of touch with those who care about you for reasons you have not stopped to consider. Psychiatrists Thomas Holmes and Richard Rahe compiled an inventory of significant life events that cause high stress, called the Holmes-Rahe Life Stress Inventory.

Military personnel and their families experience many of those events—moving, changing jobs, a loved one's chronic illness, injury, or death—at rates that far exceed what the average civilian experiences.

When you are in survival mode, it's hard to rise above the fray and take stock of where you stand with your key relationships, including the most important one: with yourself.

If you add up your score from this list and get 300 or higher, you are at a greater risk for illness manifesting in the next two years; 150–299 indicates a 50/50 risk of illness in the next two years; and a score of less than 150 predicts only a slight risk of illness. You can find the full inventory at www.stress.org/holmes-rahe-stress-inventory/. Work to reduce your score, even if it takes time to do so.

When I look over these lists, given all the transitions I've experienced and the traumas of my youth and young adulthood, I understand why I lost my way at times and was angry with the world. That's not an excuse for any pain I caused anyone, but I am acknowledging that stress creates chaos. I suspect that many of you reading this book will relate.

A vital step in **reconnecting** is taking responsibility for yourself. You must be in control of your actions and reactions—regardless of fault and disharmony around you. That's the only way you can help create the conditions for a positive outcome. Set your ego aside and be honest about your thoughts and feelings.

Beware of going for short-term fixes like drugs and alcohol. They may make you feel better in the moment, but that temporary emotional numbing is short-lived. Carefully read about the side effects and warnings associated with prescription drugs as well.

If you are depressed or having trouble adjusting to your latest transition, have the courage to reach out and get help. If you are concerned about jeopardizing your military career, consider speaking confidentially with counselors, or someone you trust. I call it releasing the air out of the balloon. Keeping everything inside is not healthy.

Do your best and do your part to always make your relationships a win/win—even if they do not turn out the way you'd hoped. Sometimes that means moving on and creating a new life for yourself. But only when we admit that things are irreparably harmed and take responsibility for our part in that will we find ourselves again.

These are all decision points. **R**ecognize that your ego, bad attitude, and unwillingness to embrace the current reality may be factors in the condition of any poor relationship. Admit your mistakes, take stock of what you want to change, and make new life choices. This step takes energy, determination, and gut-level honesty with yourself and your family and friends.

Making the shift from the battle mindset to the Warrior's Code mindset will allow you to march forward into your new life. What can you do to break the cycle that keeps you in survival mode rather than thriving mode? **First, recognize that you are a different person than you were a decade ago, last year, last month, even last week**. Goals and situations change, priorities shift, relationships are in flux, because everyone around you is changing, too.

Here is something I learned when I became a Success Principles Coach for Jack Canfield: Remember for every action, there is a response, and for every response, there is an outcome. Many times, the outcome we get is not the one we wanted or expected. Why? Because we responded in the wrong way. The problem is we always focus on the event and give it the power. It is not where the power is. The power is in our responses.

As an adult, I've always driven myself to achieve as a leader. A higher education was part of my plan, and getting advanced degrees was one of the ways I tried to prove myself. After I was awarded my master's degree, a friend of mine bet me that he would get his law degree if I would go for mine, too. We both ended up finishing our law degrees, but I decided not to practice because I was not going to live in California. I had been interested in business my whole life. Now I could apply my law degree to building that business with a special emphasis on my own organization. My military career was beginning to wind down, and I knew from years of education that it is never wasted.

At my promotion party that we held privately with some friends, a fellow officer's wife asked, "What are you going to do with your law degree?"

I responded, "Whatever I want." I had proven to myself that whatever I set my mind to, I can do if I don't give up. At fifty-one, I was now reconnecting with myself on a new level. It felt good. Change is not the end, it is a new beginning.

RECONNECTING WITH YOUR FAMILY

What wasn't going as well after I returned from my deployment and finished all my studying and hard work toward my law degree was my relationship with my wife, Denise, and our son Adam.

Denise has always been independent and has pursued her own goals as well. She's also made enormous sacrifices in her own career as a nurse. She's worked as a float nurse and in hospice and intensive care as well as at a nursing home. She was a nurse educator, and in 2016 she became a nurse practitioner. I am proud of her for her own resilience, and she is the best nurse I have ever known. She moved around all these years and plugged in using her nursing skills wherever she could in whatever part of the US we were stationed—all without complaining.

When I arrived home to Orlando from my yearlong deployment including nine months in Afghanistan, Denise and Adam met me at the airport. It was the best day of my life when I saw them again. But I bore new mental scars from a year of war. Things were not the same when I returned. My wife and son had done exactly what they were supposed to: get on with life while I was gone and survive the separation.

We talked plenty during my deployment, but the lack of physical contact drove a wedge. When I returned from deployment, I had high hopes and anticipation about how things were going to be when I got home. My immediate wants were simple: reunite with my family, get the keys to my car, pet my dog, and have a cheeseburger. I wanted to just pick up where we left off.

That did not happen.

Denise and Adam had developed their own rhythm, and that brought up my insecurity about whether I was needed and wanted. On top of that, I was facing my surgery to replace my hip while we were trying to reconnect. That made it almost impossible to focus on each other as a family because I was consumed with trying to get healthy again. Many times, I felt like a burden due to my inability to get around in my own house.

What my fantasy reunion didn't account for was that distance creates division, and we all change over time. **The reconnection we anticipate does not always unfold as we envisioned it.**

One night I finally broke down and told Denise exactly how low I was feeling. I felt disconnected from our son and her and felt like I was a huge burden. She then told me sweetly but directly that she had a routine while I was gone, but when I returned it did feel like I was in her way. She had a schedule that was working, and having a broken-down paratrooper, who appeared to be in competition with the dog on who could be the laziest, was not part of her plan.

That was the kick in the pants I needed. We found a local church we felt good about and started going to church regularly. I'd been baptized years earlier when I was at basic training at Fort Dix, New Jersey, but once I got involved with the woman who became Wife Number Two, I attended church only once in a while.

More than two decades had passed, and I wanted to be a better man for my family. I was desperate to find a way to reconnect with Denise and our eleven-year-old son, who had begun to get into a little mischief. He was happy to have me home, but I was in a haze during my recovery.

I kept thinking everything would be back to normal if Adam and I could just go out for a long run together like we used to and blow off steam and frustration. But I could no longer run. When we were in California, I got involved in Boy Scouts, outdoor events, and baseball, and helped him set up his gamer crew with some kids in the neighborhood so we could bond again.

I started actively mentoring him, and I now see the fruits of my efforts. I am pleased that even though my son now has made mistakes, he is far better adjusted than I was at his age. That goes for all my children, even though I was not able to reconnect with my adult children as solidly due to the turmoil of divorce, distance, and my own inability to communicate and get over my own issues. Life is messy, but never let others dictate your future.

About a year after my return, my wife and I did a triathlon together. We began doing more things as a family again, and we started reconnecting. We used some of the tools we learned during the Army's Strong Bonds events, where couples work through issues together. Finally, we found ourselves doing group hugs and doing little things for each other that showed our affection. Life was almost back to normal.

The important thing is that we didn't give up. **We stayed in the relationship, figured out how to nurture our love for one another, and embraced our new family dynamic.** Marriage takes work, and it takes two.

Greg Pace

Joined the Marine Corps out of high school. Served in two conflicts in Grenada. Inspector-instructor training reservists for active duty at Marine Corps headquarters. Volunteered for

Desert Storm, but was left behind at headquarters. Retired as a Captain in 1993 after twelve years of service. Currently national director of Military Veteran Affairs at DeVry University.

I was married with two stepdaughters and two daughters and a nephew living with us. I was trying to support my family and moved my family next to my brother-in-law because we couldn't afford to live in DC on a Captain's pay. I had a three-and-a-half-to-four-hour commute for two years. It's a unique life in terms of service members getting called for training and deployments. We were separated quite a bit. We did not last and wound up divorcing.

Unfortunately, I see many couples give up on each other—especially when there's been a physical or mental injury. I know from personal experience how hard it is to stay in the fight when you are in constant pain, your ego has taken a beating, and you've never fully recovered from past traumas on top of that. I know the harm it brings to all involved when we are unable to reconnect.

Todd Lewis

Director of Operations PTSD Foundation of America for the South Carolina chapter. Started with 172nd Infantry

Brigade as an enlisted man, went Airborne and became a paratrooper. Commissioned as a Second Lieutenant after Officer's School. Training support battalion. Separated from thirty-four years of continuous service, with the last fourteen and a half years active duty on July 31, 2017, in the Army. Served in Iraq in 2006 and in Afghanistan from January 2009 to January 2010. Comes from a Gold Star family with career military father and two sons currently in the military.

For me, it was difficult being out of the family. My wife did a fabulous job keeping the home fires burning, but each time it was a difficult thing to adjust to. It was disruptive when I stepped out and equally disruptive when I stepped back in. A turning point came when my twelve-year-old daughter asked, "Why are you angry all the time?" When I said that I didn't yell or show my anger, she said, "I know, Dad, but I see it in your eyes." That is when I agreed to go to some counseling sessions. Usually the six-month mark was when things boiled to the surface. I was fighting the remnants of PTSD—night terrors, nightmares, insomnia. Even a simple errand could be torturous. I had to leave Lowe's and go sit out in the car. I used to be the social butterfly, but now our roles have completely reversed. I like solitude and am not a social person. It's so important to have faith. I spend time in the Word or in prayer. Veterans have real reasons to feel abandoned. For me, solace is found in spending quiet time with God.

In my experience, troubled relationships are the number-one problem that causes us to spin out of control. In my role as an Inspector General both in Afghanistan and stateside, I often met with soldiers who had been devastated by breakups while they were deployed. The US ranks in the top ten in the world for divorces, with more than half of all marriages ending that way.

BRETT HALE

Served thirteen years in Army, half away from family during four deployments: Pentagon, Fort Benning, Iraq, Afghanistan. Retired as a Colonel in 2012. One hundred percent total and permanent disabled veteran.

Reconnecting for some veterans is impossible. I wasn't going to go chasing after family when I had four shoulder surgeries, ruptured my kidney, and had so many health problems. Family should just be there for support. My biggest escape, besides bawling my eyes out, was to go walking at a local greenway and nature park. I had to disconnect to reconnect.

You need to acknowledge your emotions and concentrate on working on *you* whenever you experience turbulence in a relationship or a breakup. Your own welfare is the most important factor in reconnecting with anyone. You can't share love and compassion if it is all bottled up inside. Become the best version of yourself, but some reflection might be giving you hints that some things need to change. It is not a gotcha, it is a wake-up call. We all need to improve.

PATRICK McGINNIS

Enlisted in the Air Force out of high school in 1980 just as the registration for the draft was mandated. Served eleven years active duty deploying satellite and microwave communications systems in support of combat communications for multiple branches and government agencies. Supported operations in Southwest Asia, Panama, South America, and Haiti. Left the Air Force after the first Gulf War to serve full time in the Air Force Air National Guard for five additional years. Now vice president of IT operations for Meridian Loyalty, a multinational corporation.

One thing I quickly learned is once you are assigned to a combat unit, you never get out of one, which was especially true for the Air Force at that time. Being deployed three of the six and a half years I was stationed in that unit certainly put a heavy burden on my eleven-year marriage. Even though I was an E-5, my top-end pay was nowhere near enough to cover all the additional expenses we encountered in my many deployments. My absences caused real financial strain for my family in an already stressful situation. The stress was compounded by the fact I could not tell anyone where I was going or why. In Panama, I spent many months there on multiple deployments. During that operation, right before Christmas, my wife learned we had launched an offensive against Noriega and the Panamanian Defense Force when she was awakened at 1:00 a.m. by a friend who called her and told her to turn on the TV. It was tough.

During all that time, she had everything regarding our family thrown into her lap while she was caring for our two sons and was forced to do her best to make ends meet so I could focus on my job. Six months after the first Gulf War ended, I left active duty to pursue a job with the Air Force Air National Guard (AFANG) in an effort to salvage my marriage and keep my career. Unfortunately for me, my decision coincided with our country's new leadership's order to reduce active-duty numbers by half. The new position I accepted in the AFANG became a primary unit to help fulfill the active-duty gaps being created because of the drawdown. In 1994 we were deployed to support the military intervention to remove the Haitian military regime of Aristide.

Fortunately for me—unlike many military veterans—I gained a marketable skill from the military in communications/computer systems. I was able to double my income the minute I walked away. But what I didn't have was the ability to check out or walk away from some of the things I had to deal with in combat situations. I deployed on the first real armed conflicts and war since Vietnam fifteen-plus years earlier. Issues like PTSD were not clearly understood, so there was no real help or discussion about it. PTSD was something you just had to deal with on your own. Over time, I learned how to deal with my issues and try to make myself a better person, father, and friend. The combat veterans over the past twenty years who have succeeded me have all dealt with a very different enemy, who used brutal and unconscionable tactics compared to the traditional warfare of armies. That coupled with the constant deployment schedules put many of them in long-term stress situations. I am relieved to know there are resources available to help them cope and recover.

Without coming to grips with whatever adversity or loss has come your way, you get stuck and cannot move forward. Playing the part of the Lone Ranger and trying to deal with everything on your own only compounds your problems.

Don't isolate yourself because you want to avoid "burdening" anyone else. A problem shared is a problem halved. The worst course of action you can take is to isolate yourself and try to deal with a major transition or trauma all alone.

And don't isolate yourself because you think you will feel less pain if it doesn't affect others. That is magical thinking.

Those who know and love you can tell when you are suffering. Learning to accept a new reality is critical for your mental health. If you ignore it, it doesn't actually go anywhere. It stays real, right outside the door you close on it, lurking until you deal with it.

I recognize looking back that my hip replacement not only sent me into depression, but it also dinged my self-image. I'd thought of myself as a warrior/athlete, and now both parts of my self-image were in question. For a while I allowed my own inner critic to do a number on me and spent far too much time ruminating about all the things I could no longer do instead of figuring out how to be the best "new" me. The result was I pushed my family away because I did not want them to see my weaknesses or vulnerability.

It does not matter if you're in the military or not. There are three truths I believe are important in reconnecting:

- The adjustment never goes as we think it will, so stay at it.
- It can and will be a difficult time, and it takes time to adjust.
- Any time we jump out of or back into a relationship, emotions run high. Be prepared for that reality. Storybook reunions only happen in storybooks. Real life is messy.

Reuniting with and reconnecting with ourselves and others is beneficial in so many ways. After any type of traumatic experience, your mind needs to regroup. Not only do you have to come to grips with the situation you're in, so do those around you.

SHERRY LEWIS

Wife of Todd Lewis, an army veteran with thirty-four years of service, and has two sons in the military. She started a wellness practice that helps veterans ease stress and anxiety after she saw what her husband was going through with PTSD.

We have been married for twenty-two years. There was a lot of stress and tension that first year he was back. I didn't know how I could help. It's so hard because you don't know exactly what they have dealt with. It definitely made a big difference in our life to be able to reconnect. We began running together. It was great to run through the country away from the crazy hustle and bustle. Part of what my husband needed was to be able to have time to himself where he was able to be alone and decompress. One of the things that was so ingrained in us was that we had to go through traditional routes for everything we needed. I see so much more hope and success for people if they don't give up and start looking at the alternative routes. At least give it a try.

One of the big areas of disconnection comes when we each have different expectations. When you've been away from your loved ones for an extended period of time, it's understandable that they would want you to jump back into life as it was before.

That's not realistic. You all need space to get used to your new reality. Part of loving yourself is tapping into what you need and gently communicating that to your family. If you need quiet time to yourself at a certain time of the day, let your significant other know that. If being around a lot of people jangles your nerves or being in a place where there are a lot of loud noises puts you on edge, speak up.

Hitting bumps and roadblocks during a transition does not mean giving up. Learning to accept some things are absolutes is healthy. Once you do that and try to help your loved ones do so as well, you are more prepared to deal with the new you—whoever that might be.

RECONNECTING WITH FRIENDS

When you are in the military, you move around a lot. It can be tempting to shed relationships just for the sake of moving on. The constant state of flux causes us to be present where we are, but our lack of solid roots does not encourage us to build long-term connections.

New schools, new friends, new experiences, new residences, new sports teams, and new work associates. Denise and I learned to tell ourselves it was just another adventure. We would find new restaurants to go to, make new friends, and learn about our new location. Some friends have become long term, but many were just acquaintances. You are in a constant state of change that makes you adopt coping mechanisms to reconnect over and over without it being a big deal.

As I've gotten older, I've learned the important benefits of staying in touch with friends, mentors, and colleagues. **Maintaining healthy relationships from your past can provide important clues to your future and help ground you. Those relationships help remind you of how far you've come.** When I wrote this book, it brought back memories of people who made substantial differences in my life, of happy times and heartbreak, but it also brought healing.

My early life as a fighter came full circle in 2015 when I traveled to the inaugural Liberty Taekwondo Championship in Hinesville, Georgia. Almost eighty commissioned and noncommissioned officers, many of whom had won medals in taekwondo as members of the US teams from different branches of the military—the majority US Army—gathered over that mid-September weekend near Fort Stewart to celebrate the thirtieth anniversary of the inaugural US Army taekwondo team being established. I'd had only sporadic contact with my teammates through the years.

In 1985 I was part of a trio of enlisted men at Fort Bragg,

North Carolina, assigned to the 82nd Airborne Division and 18th Airborne Corps, who united to comprise the first taekwondo team to wear the US Army colors in a national competition. At first glance, we couldn't have been more different: Pedro Laboy and Rafael Medina were both from Puerto Rico, and I was a white boy from Moberly, Missouri.

"It wasn't until we brought home medals that our commanding officer realized we were serious about this sport, and we weren't just looking for a reason to get out of our regular duties," Medina said when we reminisced at the reunion.

Eventually, Medina coached both the Army Armed Forces taekwondo team and the World Class Athlete Program (WCAP) Armed Forces team from 1996 to 2000. Grand Masters Medina and Laboy, both now retired from military service, went on to be participants in the World Class Athlete Program.

At the September celebration, many of the sport's most celebrated soldier-athletes, like Bongseok Kim, president of the Taekwondo Committee of the Conseil International du Sport Militaire (also known as the International Military Sports Council), congregated along with many of the other past fighters of the Army teams to recall our shared history and discuss how to rekindle the passion for taekwondo in today's military that our pioneering team had ignited.

During that weekend, as a group whose motto is "One Team One Fight, One Team One Family," we agreed to form an alumni association to promote the popularity of the sport.

My teammate Medina was elected the inaugural president of the fledgling organization.

Being a part of that team gave us a chance to be a part of something that was bigger than ourselves. It taught me that you can overcome obstacles no matter what you face.

Reconnecting with friends with whom I share such a powerful bond ended up being one of the best actions I've taken in a long time. It served as a reminder of my best self and how important long-term friendships are.

So what steps do you need to take to reconnect?

- **Get back in touch with yourself.** Use prayer, meditation, time with friends and loved ones, vacation, and brief getaways. In the end, only when you focus on your responses can you hope to create the results and outcomes that you desire. Trying to change everybody else around you never works. Over the past three years leading up to my retirement and next chapter, I've taken several steps that I never imagined would be part of my routine. My goals and aspirations are written on my bathroom mirror so that I see them first thing when I wake up.
- **Put time into figuring out where you are in life right at this moment.**

- **Don't be afraid to share feelings of insecurity in an important relationship**. That's not being weak. That's being real.
- **Reconnect** with your family, your friends, and your pets. Be honest about what you are thinking and feeling. Once you do that, you are more prepared to deal with the new you.
- **Never underestimate the importance of long-term relationships. Keep in touch.** As human beings, we are created to need connection. Positive connections help us reconnect with our best selves and with those we love the most in meaningful ways.

STEP 3

RESET YOUR MIND

There is no way around this. When we come back, we must all **hit the reset button on our mind.** We have seen things, heard things, experienced things that have been seared into our cells. We have learned different ways of behaving that come naturally now even though we don't need to act that way in our civilian life at work and in relationships.

Even if you were never deployed to a war zone, as a member of the military you develop a battle mindset. It comes with the territory. **What worked in the military does not always translate to civilian life.** What we were rewarded for in service to our country may not bring the same approval outside the Air Force, Army, Coast Guard, Marine Corps, and Navy—institutions that value a certain protocol and mindset.

We have built up many strengths but may need to use them differently. Switch out military protocol for the Warrior's Code, which has "your six," and your back. Hit reset in your mind in order to be open to learning a new way of living. Like the military, the Code is accepting new recruits who want to win.

Anxiety, worry, stress, fear, anger, and bad attitudes—in other words, stinking thinking—can turn your mind into a combat zone. We don't need to be there. Opt out and rethink the sources of your negativity. If you suffer from post-traumatic stress syndrome—and coming out of the military many of us do, although we may not want to admit it—your own thoughts can trigger a flood of negative emotions that cripple your efforts to move forward.

Post-traumatic stress syndrome is a real disorder, and you may need professional help with it. Reset your mind and get that help. You are not giving in; you're simply *not* giving up.

Alter, amend, transform, correct, improve, renew, and reorganize your mind. Whatever it takes to generate a positive mindset, you must do. Stinking thinking does not leave on its own. It stinks up the whole person, your home, your backyard, your relationships, your work. Surface fixes like distraction don't work. You need to focus on what you want in order to shift from the battle mindset to a positive mindset.

This is one battle you cannot afford to lose. And you won't if you commit yourself to the Warrior's Code.

To transform your mind to that of a powerful warrior in civilian life requires your best effort, your full attention, and your constant vigilance. Not hypervigilance, which is a remnant of your military service and is an exaggerated state of intensity that can cause exhaustion and anxiety, a high responsiveness to stimuli, and a constant scanning of the environment. I mean civilian vigilance, which means keep a careful watch for dangers or difficulties.

Making this shift will not be easy. It will take time, training, and dedication. This conscious shift in how you think and control your thoughts can radically change your life. No matter your circumstances, it is within your control.

Arlene Marshman

Raised in Puerto Rico. Her father was in the Air Force. She signed up with the Navy upon high school graduation because the Air Force recruiting office was closed that day. In communications since 1979. Stationed in Italy, Charleston, Bermuda, Iceland, and then Pensacola. Retired E-6 Petty Officer First Class.

I had no clue what to do when I left the Navy. I didn't know what the whole civilian culture was. My skills didn't translate to the civilian world. I applied for a job as a flight attendant. I was hired by Piedmont Airlines, but weeks after I got hired they were bought out by US Air. My new husband was a Navy officer who'd gotten out at the same time. We were both unemployed. We moved to DC, because that's where his family was, and we knew contractors were there. We didn't know how to make our way, but luckily my husband got hired right away by a contractor, and I did, too, because I still had a valid top-secret clearance and expertise in communications. It was a confusing and difficult time. My first job after Navy communications was answering the phone. That was it.

When I wound up in that apartment in a dangerous area south of Atlanta during one of my last assignments, I got really down. I mean really, really down. I started questioning why I was on this earth. It was time to pivot and make a change. My mind, body, and spirit were aching for it. **You will know when you reach that point, and that moment is defining. Give yourself a chance to see your future in a different way even if that takes a little time to figure it out.**

My request for compassionate reassignment to Florida to tend to my elderly mom who had been diagnosed with cancer had been denied. I was worried about her and wanted to spend time with her while I still could. We had to give up a beautiful home in California where we'd made lots of friends, and my wife and son had settled in Orlando to be near my mother while I was assigned to Fort Gillem. What was my purpose as a son and husband if I couldn't support my family during these transitions?

I was lonely.

Once again, I was separated from my family, and I felt guilty that my wife was shouldering a burden on her own as she had had to do so many times when I was away. I didn't feel like making much of an effort to make friends at work on the base. *What was the point?*

Besides being depressed and lonely, I was angry that I had to be separated from my family, and the distance only made it worse.

Night after night I'd sit in a chair with my gun aimed at the door, unnerved by the frequent sound of gunfire nearby. That would trigger the same kind of hypervigilance I felt throughout the nine months I was deployed in Afghanistan. My nerves were shot.

All that time to myself left me way too much time to think about my mistakes, failed relationships, and financial missteps. On top of that, the leaves changing and dropping off reminded me that the holidays were coming, and there I sat in what I called the Hobo Hotel, with nothing more than a small chair, a storage container with a lamp on it, my TV, and a small single bed. Being stuck in that apartment by myself left me feeling lower than a snake's belly in a wagon rut. I got so low that I started worrying that Denise might be thinking about divorcing me.

Three strikes, and you are out, Buddy, I told myself glumly.

I had become my own worst enemy.

Finally, I decided something had to give.

ALBERT AMADOR

Father was a Marine in the Korean War and did three tours of Vietnam. One of fourteen children raised in the barrio in San Diego. Ran away at age fourteen and joined Marines at age twenty, spending fourteen years, first as a water-purification specialist and then as a marksman instructor and a member of the Marine Corps Rifle and Pistol Team. One of the first to learn how to pilot a drone. Served in Desert Storm and in Afghanistan in 2010–2011. Did career planning and was a readiness trainer for NCOs getting ready to deploy to Afghanistan. Retired in April 2016 with twenty-six years of service.

My first marriage was at age twenty-two. When I got back from Desert Storm, she was living with another man. The divorce rate was so high at Twentynine Palms that there was an entire theatre being used for a class on divorce. Through my first transition after a draw-down, I got divorced a second time. When I came back from Desert Storm, I took a fishing pole, camping equipment, and a bottle of Jack Daniels with me to the mountains after my second divorce. I had thirty days leave and camped off the grid to regroup and think. I reset my values to establish what kind of person I wanted to be and what I wanted to do. Then in 2004 a buddy told me about Army National Guard. I realized if I put in six more years I could retire. I have a Purple Heart and got bumped up to 80 percent disability. Now with my wife, Carla, I have twin daughters. We try to keep everything positive. I went to work immediately when I got out of the military. I got hired for robotics with Uber.

I have always loved reading, and I reached for some of the

self-help books lining my shelf. The more I read about the importance of rest, the deeper I delved into the powerful role your mind plays in your well-being.

My thoughts were always racing. Each of us has approximately twenty to eighty thousand thoughts a day. This next bit of information stunned me: scientists estimate that ***up to 80 percent of those thoughts are negative***—the coulda, shoulda, woulda kind of thoughts.

I was the king of that kind of thinking.

Reading through the research, I became convinced that **negative thoughts disrupt your brain's ability to rest. To get rest, you must develop the ability to quiet your mind.** I'd been guilty of ruminating over negative events in my life, which clouded my ability to live in the present and focus on the good. That habit made it impossible for me to get much sleep. In fact, I couldn't remember the last time I'd gotten any solid rest.

Start paying attention to what you focus on. Scientists have proven that if you constantly think about what's going wrong in your life and all your problems, your brain will rewire itself to put more attention on the negative events in your life. When you put out that kind of negative energy, you attract more of it and it literally drains you. Learning to stamp out ANTS (automatic negative thoughts) takes persistence.

I realized that I'd developed the bad habit of focusing on the negative. For one thing, my job as an Inspector General meant that I was listening to other people's problems every day. Plus, I was spending a lot of time dwelling in the past, beating myself up for things I had no control over as well as the things I was responsible for.

JASON DODGE

When veterans get out of the military, it doesn't matter what your rank was. You have an identity crisis. I used to be Sergeant Dodge. I really missed being part of a team and being part of something that was bigger than myself.

Once I resolved to change my mind—at least the way I'd been using it—I devoted my off-hours to reading positive affirmations and self-help books. I reached out to a writer with a sixty-five-thousand-word manuscript I'd been working on over the years. Originally, I started writing as a way to process my anger and grief over the many traumas and losses I'd endured throughout my life. To my surprise, she thought I had a story worth telling. Her faith in me fueled my determination to radically shift my thinking, even if I couldn't change my circumstance. That resulted in the book *Step Out, Step Up: Lessons Learned from a Lifetime of Transitions and Military Service.*

TIM BOONE, PHD

Some people join the military not for the best of reasons. When they come out, it's not like they are suddenly this wonderful, whole person. They are messed up just like the rest of us. To reset your mind, you've got to forgive yourself for mistakes you've made, for people you've hurt. The question becomes how do I take charge of my life? You've got to find out who you really are. You've got to look at the below-the-line stuff that you don't want to acknowledge.

Six months after I started working with her on this project, my attitude had shifted significantly. Instead of thinking about all my problems and frustrations, my thoughts were consumed with how I could use my life experiences to help others. Each time I'd make the six-hour drive down I-75 to Orlando to see my family, I used the time to record my thoughts. I initially intended them as lessons for my teenage son Adam, but soon realized that anyone who desired positive change could benefit from them.

As I focused on gratitude and concentrated on noticing the good in my life rather than the bad, I went to the chain of command and once again made my request for a compassionate reassignment. I was with a medical command, and they listened and understood my situation. My request was granted. It felt like a miracle. After almost a year, I was allowed to join my family in Orlando.

I made the decision that I was going to take control of my own future. If something was going to change, I was going to have to be the one to take the steps. I was going to work on myself: how I dealt with adversity, how I dealt with the past, how I planned to remove anxiety and worry about the future from the equation.

Over the last three years since I've been writing my two books and planning my transition to civilian life, I began meditating, praying, and using the exercise of envisioning success and happiness to start my day. I learned from taking Jack Canfield's *The Success Principles* training that a big part of success is focusing on positive thoughts.

I took another big step toward retraining my brain when I did something I never imagined myself doing: I hired a meditation coach. Now each morning when things are not too hectic, I take the quiet part of the day to think about what I am grateful for, contemplate my most important goals, and concentrate on all the good that it is in my life.

The change I am seeing is indescribable. So many doors have opened and so many positive things have happened. My path of helping others has been a great choice. I have improved my chances of higher income, and I got rid of the baggage of the past. I invested in myself and my future, which has opened up great opportunities. My eyes have been opened to a whole new world, and I want others to experience that.

Exercise, positive affirmations, reading quotes, and writing down my visions of what I want not only my transition to look like, but what I want in every area of my life, have become my laser focus. Each of these steps builds on the other to create change and triumphant transition.

So how do you reset your mind? Here are some of the steps that have helped me radically change and achieve a warrior's mindset:

- **Challenge your negative thoughts.** Ask yourself, *Is this true?* For example, if you are having trouble with your spouse or significant other, write down the things you love about that person and read them early in the morning and again before you go to bed. Pretty soon you'll find yourself focusing on the positive rather than what you dislike.
- **Start your day with meditation, prayer, and envisioning what you want in your life.** I put together a vision board that I keep in my office. It's a visual representation of what I want in my life.
- **Keep a journal to help you process your thoughts and feelings.** Share your story with a trusted friend or loved one. If you bottle everything up inside, eventually your frustration and anger will boil to the surface.
- **Learn to pay attention to your breathing.** For me, that simple step was one of the most important new habits I formed. It helps me to relax and rest.

- **Exercise.** Getting your heart pumping releases endorphins. Even though I'm officially 80 percent disabled, I recently successfully tested for my fourth-degree black belt in taekwondo. Find a way to work out despite your limitations. If possible, get out in nature and contemplate the beauty around you. Our bodies crave negative ions, which are produced by large bodies of the water and by forests. Think about it. That's why vacations by the sea or in the mountains leave you feeling refreshed. In fact, in Japan, for the past three decades doctors have looked into all the health benefits of spending time in the woods. Studies show that a weekend in the woods lowers your blood pressure and produces endorphins and boosts your well-being significantly for the next thirty days.
- **Read positive affirmations.** Words matter. Everything from what you read to the movies or television shows you watch to the music you listen to matters. In fact, a study showed that famous singers who sang sad songs night after night versus those whose music tended to be happier lived an average of twenty years less than their peers and were more likely to die of suicide.
- **Pay attention to your environment.** For example, your sense of smell is powerful when it comes to

conjuring up memories. Use essential oils that smell good to you and remind you of happy times. When I do get the chance to go to Hawaii to my house there, I like to use that time to unwind, reset my mind, and enjoy nature at its best. The beauty of the island is breathtaking and really rejuvenates me. I also enjoy playing music that calms me. Studies show that music that you enjoy can significantly boost your mood. For example, I love listening to what we call "cigar box music," because it reminds me of my Missouri roots and happy days fishing with my grandpa.

- **Be mindful of your self-talk**. If you wouldn't say the things to your best friend that you say to yourself, you need to change the way you talk to an important person in your life: YOU!
- **Do not be afraid to ask for help**. You may need professional help to navigate especially tough times. When I was retiring I met with a psychologist at the VA. He offered me a prescription, but I turned down the offer. I told him I'd developed my own way of coping with past traumas through the intentional hard reset on my mind. For some people, drugs may be warranted, but in my case, I knew I'd already conquered the toughest part of that battle and didn't want drugs to mask my feelings.

- **Focus on looking for the good in each day**. Write down five things you are grateful for each day and review your list before you go to sleep. Gratitude activates the neurotransmitter dopamine. Gratitude and a strong, positive warrior's mindset are the foundation for resilience. You will never be sorry if you take this path. The rewards are exponential.

STEP 4

REMOVE NEGATIVITY

You already know you must reset your mind in order to be resilient and adjust to your new life. Much of what that involves is removing negativity. Let's talk about negativity and your mind first and then negativity in your life.

Negative beliefs come from small talk with ourselves that is not factual. Our own opinions of ourselves affect our feelings and lead to our own criticism of who we are, and we stonewall any good. **We move to the fight-or-flight response only because it is all we know.**

Our minds can take us where we want to go. If you only think failure, it will give you that. If you only think that you are cheated, it will give you that. If you only think you are inferior, it is happy to oblige. What if you replaced those thoughts? **If you only think success, it will give you that. If you only think exceptional, it will give you that.** We have all heard the words "garbage in, garbage out." With our minds, that holds true.

Dr. Daniel Amen coined the term ANTS, meaning Automatic Negative Thoughts, in the early 1990s after a hard day at the office with suicidal patients, teenagers in turmoil, and a married couple who hated each other. When he got home he found thousands of ants in his kitchen and made the connection that his patients' brains were also infested with "ANTS" that were robbing them of their peace of mind. He is the author of ten books, including *Change Your Brain, Change Your Life,* which is part of our challenge in transitioning from the military to civilian life.

I don't want to requisition Dr. Amen's ANTS brainstorm as if it is proprietary to *Warrior's Code 001*. It's not, and versions of it are available to all on many websites and in print. But I want you to know what you are up against when it comes to these Automatic Negative Thoughts, because they do tend to invade like an army and colonize in your head, making it difficult for you to even enjoy a sandwich without having them walk all over it.

AUTOMATIC NEGATIVE THOUGHTS (ANTS)

- **"Always and never" thinking.** This is when you believe words like "always, never, no one, everyone, every time, everything" as if they are absolutes, when they are only generalizations based on one or two examples. An example is "I can never do anything right, according to you," based on one comment offered as sincere feedback from a family member.
- **Focusing on the negative.** Say you are given a critique in a work review that has examples of supe-

rior and subpar contributions. If you only focus on the negative comments, you are selling yourself short.

- **Fortune telling.** If you tend to predict the worst possible outcome for a situation, you are a worrier, not a warrior. Sometimes good things happen too.
- **Mind reading.** Very few people are actual mind readers, and I can guarantee you are not one of them. If you believe that you know what another person is thinking—even though they haven't told you and you didn't ask—and what they are thinking is not good, you might want to stomp on those ANTS.
- **Thinking with your feelings.** This is especially hazardous when you are angry, depressed, lonely, or feel betrayed and taken advantage of. Don't believe negative feelings without questioning them. There could be a perfectly reasonable explanation for your negativity, like you need a nap because you were up all night fighting a war that was no longer being fought.
- **Guilt beatings.** Stop whipping yourself with words like "should, must, ought" or "have to." You don't "have to." You have choices. Make a good one. If you already made a bad one, leave it where it lies. It's not going to get better by you dragging it around with you.

- **Labeling.** You probably know what this feels like because you may very well have been labeled by others at some point in your life. Or maybe you were the labeler, which often means "bully." If so, stop—and apologize when needed. If not, don't bully yourself with labels. Nobody is only one thing; no label can encompass a human's entire being.
- **Personalization.** How many times have you heard the phrase "Don't take it personally"? We almost always do anyway. But sometimes it's just not about you, so don't make the leap from innocent comment to negative comment unless you can back it up with evidence.
- **Blame.** This is one of those red fire ANTS that bites, injects poison, swells, itches, and leaves a scar. Stop blaming your own issues and faults on someone else. Remember, blame BITES.

LOVE YOUR MIND

What kind of things are you telling yourself? Are you beating yourself up? Labeling? Generalizing? Thinking with your feelings? We all do, so don't beat yourself up even more. Just start noticing, and one by one, stamp out those automatic negative thoughts.

Quiet those voices that say you or someone else or what you have or do is not good enough and change the narrative. We will all have bad days or bad moments, but in the end, we control what we think if we have functioning brains. We have a choice in what we tell ourselves. If we need help in making decisions at times because that is not the case, then do not try and make decisions without input from others—which is why we must surround ourselves with people with some common sense who are more positive than negative.

Removing negativity begins with awareness and some subtle but constant tweaks. I have done all of these, and guess what? They work. Do not give up the first time you try and fail at banishing negativity. It is a process of persistence that pays off.

What we put into our heads is what becomes our truth. Breaking the cycle of negativity—woe is me—and putting the words "I can't" or "it is impossible" into your mind only makes things harder. Instead, replace negative thoughts with positive ones.

Think about what you do have, and everything you are grateful for when you start thinking negatively. Being grateful for anything in life changes our thinking. What makes you happy? Whatever it is, focus on it. All of us have had those rough spots where we were in a funk. **Our minds will cultivate what we plant, so pull the weeds and tend to your garden of thoughts.** Gratitude is the one thing I learned that connects the head with the heart in a better way. Even after failure or disappointment. Even after a relationship gone wrong or a tough situation.

Many things in life are temporary, and our minds can make it better or worse. We are in charge of that message. Use meditation and bring your subconscious mind into the change you want to see. I always thought meditation was some strange stuff that was just chanting and incoherent garbage. What I learned is that meditation works to build a healthy subconscious that spills over to our conscious self. I am eternally grateful and thankful to Sabine Buhlmann of Life Coaching and Meditation, who helped me begin my journey into deeper meditation and taught me the basics of calming my mind. Through my company, My Silver Boots, LLC, I am planning retreats in Florida and Hawaii where the basics of the Warrior's Code curriculum can be learned.

The other wonderful thing about meditation is that it centers us. We can have the tendency to have external things control what is going on with us. When we turn it inward and begin to work on ourselves, we find new resilience we did not realize we had. You are in charge of your thinking. You just have to begin to do it a different way.

Ask for encouragement from those around you. Humor in a situation also takes down stress levels. Give it time, start right now, and do not give up on yourself. Understand that the wiring may take a little time to adjust to the new you. It is okay and you will toggle back and forth, but be aware of it, catch yourself, and keep going. The rewards change us, and everyone around you will notice. When they start telling you or implying that you are different somehow, in a good way, you know you are on the right track. You are removing the negative and becoming positively more YOURSELF.

LOVE YOUR BODY

When I was in the 82nd Airborne, we would have jumps late at night and then start a road march for fifteen miles deep in the North Carolina pines back to our base. If a guy was top fit, he could carry his heavy rucksack, and would shred it all the way back to the base. Others would struggle, get blisters, become dehydrated, and would need intravenous fluids to make it, and some would not make it at all. Over time and with *doing* it gets easier.

It takes three things to be able to perform at your peak:

1. You have to work to be the best.
2. You have to have a rhythm and the right mindset.
3. You have to have heart when you're hurting and hit the physical or mental wall.

It was the same thing being a taekwondo athlete. If you did not train constantly on the techniques to win, you would not win. You had to have exact timing to go on the offensive or defensive at the right moment. You had to get into a groove, and when it hurt, you had to learn to block it out and push beyond your own limits to win.

That is what separates the first place from the first loser in competition.

SHERRY LEWIS

We both had physical struggles when my husband returned. We worked with a friend who trains people to breathe to learn how we could use breathing to control things: reduce anxiety and stress, slow heart rate down. We did this training for two or three months, breathing down to the abdomen. That is something that I still use to this day quite frequently. It works nicely with nutritional work as well as emotional work to destress the body. Deep breathing is also a way of being in control.

We decide if we are going to exercise and eat right and take care of our body. No matter what shape our body is in from the visible and invisible wounds of war, any trauma or event in life, it is still ours to take care of. Every story is different, and everybody is, too. It is up to you to take care of what you have, and **we must engage our mind and spirit to help us be our best physical selves.**

Do not give your body negative garbage that makes it sick. Do not make up reasons that you can't be as fit as you can be given any physical limitations that you must accept. Do not blame others for the condition of your body. Do not beat yourself up for not exceeding your expectations if you have done all that you can do. Love your body.

Once I looked up the word *disabled* in the dictionary. The dictionary defined disabled as *useless, mangled, run down. Worn out, weakened, impotent, paralyzed, decrepit, laid up. Done for*.

I did not like those words. But the dictionary definition reminds me that we must overcome feeling less of a person if we do have a disability.

I am not disabled. I have a disability. I am alive no matter what my physical capability at any given moment. Check your pulse right now and marvel at how powerful it is. We are all miracles, and there is a reason you are here.

Your body may not be the temple it once was, but love heals. Once you learn to love yourself, people will take notice, open up, and love you back. Remove any negative thoughts about your body. It has had enough pain and suffering. Be firm but gentle when you tell it what to do. Eventually, it will tell itself what to do and your brain won't be so involved. Count on it. Your body has carried you many miles.

LOVE YOUR SPIRIT

You are either religious or not. That is a choice, and I am not in the business of converting people to anything. Our spirit is not just about religion. Our spirit is within us. It is our ability to believe in something larger than ourselves. Having a spirit of cooperation, a spirit of desire to make the best of things, and a spirit of strength by being the best person we can be is the warrior spirit you should adopt if you do not have that already.

Many of us are what I call "program smart." We act all proper in spirit when we are at church, and then we are angry on the way home in the car. We can be hypocritical in our path of spirit because we say we believe, but the truth is we do not live what we preach. A strong warrior's spirit helps us conquer challenges in every area of our life. It is that anchor that helps us remember that there is a big world out there. Take a look at the sky. It is bigger than us. Think about how many grains of sand there are. We are but one small being in this amazing universe, but we are each unique and still matter.

I pay attention to nature and the world around me. I have always been fascinated with the ocean and rivers: the ability to cut canyons through rock over the course of millions of years, the power of the waves and the creatures that live within the ocean that we are still discovering.

Our spirit is tied to it all. It is proven that positive energy helps things grow. Adversely, negative energy affects growth the opposite way. I am a believer of a Higher Power. Spirit is energy from outside in and inside out. The spirit will never give up on you regardless of those who may have moved on without you. The spirit lights up what makes you feel alive. The spirit lifts others up.

Make your warrior's spirit feel comfortable. Give it some space to grow. Feed it. Talk to it. Share it. Lots of people could benefit from your positive spirit. Raise your colors and keep them flying. Your spirit represents you even when you are not there. When people say, "Your presence was missed," they mean the spirit you bring with you.

UNITING MIND, BODY, AND SPIRIT

The positive union of mind, body, and spirit is a winning combination. If we strive to master all of them, we live a more resilient life. We are better prepared for what life throws at us. I learned early in my taekwondo life that we are always working to improve in all three areas. Master instructors understand and have devoted their life work to this triad. This, along with the 7 Vital Steps to Resiliency, is the recipe to become the most resilient warrior you can be.

Jim Rohn says, "You can't hire someone else to do your push-ups for you." That does not have to be a physical thing. It is also a mental and spiritual thing. You have to apply what is shared to be resilient in transition and in life. I strive to live the Warrior's Code every day.

If you want more ideas for a triumphant transition, sign up for the Warrior's Code 100 Days of Transition, available on my website at www.mark.green. There you can find a place to share your story and connect with the Warrior's Code community.

One small hint in eliminating the negative: check your ego at the door. I know it is hard. Many veterans have big egos. We do not like to think we are affected by piddling actions of others. We can find ourselves heading into negative territory when we bump up against common situations in the civilian world where there is no prescribed process. The Warrior's Code means constantly learning to deal with new or existing issues. Have the courage to ask for help if you don't know how to navigate and feel like you've ventured into enemy territory.

Attitude is like a rocket or a rock. Your attitude determines your altitude, and it will lift you up or cause you to fall.

You won't effectively deal with problems with a sour attitude and a chip on your shoulder because of ego. When negativity enters the mind, it stifles our ability to find creative solutions.

JACLYN PETERS

I was in a toxic relationship shortly before I got out of the Marine Corps. The guy was sweet but had no goals, no idea, no plans. I already had everything planned. He had nothing. I knew the first year of transition was going to be a rough year and you need a good support system. He needed to step up or get out. He didn't step up. The first year, there are serious life changes in every aspect: you move, get a new job, have to get used to being a civilian. You have to have somebody on your side who will raise you up, not pull you down. I didn't think it was being selfish to eliminate the negative distraction that I had control over.

At times negativity might become a coping mechanism. You may default to negative emotions, which feel like part of survival. Flying the f-bomb becomes a habit in response to stress.

I understand that anger is a normal human emotion. What I'm suggesting though is that in order to tap into our warrior's spirit, we need to learn to remove ourselves from anger-provoking negative situations, negative people, negative news outlets, and negative environments. **Start living a life where you can flourish and be nourished by choosing to surround yourself with the good in life.** This critical step is one you must take in order to achieve remarkable resilience.

One of the biggest pitfalls I've witnessed among my military brothers and sisters and fellow veterans is falling into the trap of misbehavior. Most of us who join the military tend to be type-A thrill seekers who love a challenge. The flip side of that is that type of personality can make you prone to high-risk behavior that gets the adrenaline pumping.

As an Inspector General both in Afghanistan and stateside, I can tell you that extramarital affairs (whether physical or emotional or online), abuse of alcohol and drugs (prescription and illegal), gambling and sexual addictions, and other harmful habits can quickly send you spiraling out of control and destroy your health and relationships.

If you are experiencing these types of issues, there is help. Confide in someone you can trust to guide you the right way, the Warrior's Code way. That word *trust* is important. Just telling a friend who is in the same boat won't likely yield the change you are seeking. **You may end up dealing with something you cannot fix, and when that happens, you need to reach out.** Don't try and bottle it up. It will only make matters worse.

You cannot hide bad habits forever, and those closest to you are not mind readers. Bad news does not get better with time. **You will find help only after you ask for it, or someone sees that you need it and you agree.**

Find that excitement in positive pursuits. Decide to devote yourself to encouraging those around you. Get in the habit of looking for the good and offering sincere compliments.

Okay, let's agree that we have all had negativity drive decisions in our lives at times. If you think about the outcomes that brought, I will bet they were never good. If you sense negativity creeping back in like the enemy sneaking into camp, nip it in the bud. Thinking positively while going through tough times can make it easier to get through.

I did not know how to change. No one had ever taught me how to tame the negativity monster. I figured out how to slay that fire-breathing dragon that threatened to destroy everything in its path by creating the 7 Steps, which have armed me with the positivity I need to combat whatever comes my way.

Revisiting what I shared earlier in the book, a formula in Jack Canfield's book *The Success Principles* is **E + R= O**: Events plus Response equals Outcome. For every event in our lives, we get a choice on how we respond.

This one principle has helped me to slow down and make better choices. To be in more control of the outcome by being more aware of my own responses. Removing anxiety about the future comes from taking action and from knowledge replacing fear. Learn how to relax your mind so you can remove negativity and replace it with positive affirmations, faith, and daily habits that will replace the old ones.

I have worked with professionals from New York to California. I have surrounded myself with positive people who believe in me, and I have pursued positive environments. When that happens, you gain confidence in yourself.

So how do you remove negativity? Here are some of the steps that have helped me.

- **Recognize triggers for negative emotions** and enlist those closest to you to help you avoid them.
- **Surround yourself with people who are on a similar path.** Look for people you can encourage and who encourage you. The work of Jane Dutton, professor of

psychology at the University of Michigan, demonstrates that we learn and adapt better and are more resilient the more we experience positive moments with each other during the course of each day. In other words, be kind and look for others who return your kindness. Dutton explains that positive interactions at work and home are major contributors to our overall happiness. Several studies point to a lack of kindness as a major predictor of whether couples will stay together. Positive, meaningful relationships tend to stick in our minds. For example, when I began concentrating on the wonderful interactions I'd had over the years with different mentors and friends, it helped me remember my best moments and aspire to have more of those.

- **Ask for help.** Do not be afraid to ask for help. The very point at which you feel out of control is the very point you need to reach out to someone. Avoiding these issues only makes things worse. Professional help may be needed and should not be avoided. Know that negativity can bring us right to the bottom. **If you find yourself there with no way out, I am asking that you make this one phone call to the Veteran Crisis Line at 1-800-273-8255 and press 1.** Then tell me later that it was our book that led you to make the call, so I know I made a difference. **If you're not a veteran, you can call the same National Suicide Prevention Lifeline at the number above, but you don't have to press 1.**

- **Laugh.** I am not kidding about this. It is no joke. Look for the humor in your situation. Who doesn't have problems? You gotta take life with a grain of salt or a spoonful of sugar, whichever makes you happier. It can be bitter. But we have the choice to lighten up. Follow the light. Laugh.
- **Practice gratitude.** Gratitude and a positive attitude are the foundation for resilience. I practice this while driving to work. I learned as a Success Principles Coach to be grateful for everything. I noticed that when I did this, it changed my mood. It made it better. I started the day off with a better disposition.
- **Actively practice compassion and look for ways to help others.**

When I was busy throwing a pity party for one, I had no room for anybody else. Once I opened my eyes to what was going on around me, I discovered I had a lot to offer others if I'd just stop being so self-focused.

Shortly after I decided to reach out, I noticed a post on Twitter by a veteran in Houston who was getting ready to have surgery and commented that he had no one who would care if he made it through or not. Nobody had responded to his mournful statement. That made me sad, so I reached out. I learned that he'd battled drug addictions, had lost his job and his apartment, and that his wife had left him. He had struggled with suicidal thoughts.

Over the past three years, I've maintained close contact with him and helped connect him with resources from an iPad to an apartment. He's got a good job and a new place. He bought a car and has a new girlfriend. Recent studies prove that the happiest people are those who give to others and have a high level of empathy. One of the experts in this area is Corey Keyes, a founding fellow of Life University's Center for Compassion, Integrity and Secular Ethics and a sociology professor at Emory University in Atlanta. Keyes, who came from a similar background as me and openly talks about his struggles with depression, has spent the past two decades examining the relationship between flourishing and mental health.

Having a positive attitude has allowed me to do my job with great outcomes and to teach and train others that with certain principles in place they can change their own lives as well.

STEP 5

RESOLVE ISSUES

In the three years since I began contemplating retiring from the military and what my next mission would be, I've had a host of issues I needed to face: from whether to go for my next promotion and break a promise to my wife and son in the process, to taking a gamble on being a vetrepreneur despite my less than stellar track record when risking being my own boss, to accepting my role of caretaker of my frail mom, whose dementia has left her combative and angry at the world, including me.

During my thirty-four years in the service, I've met many men and women who, like me, joined the military hoping to find a better life and structure. When you come from a chaotic background, your problems on the home front don't magically disappear when you sign up. No matter where you are in the world, you still carry baggage from the past as well as any current problems or challenges.

Nobody likes kitchen patrol (KP) duty. Cleaning up a mess is never fun. But I realized ruminating over my frustrations over past relationships that had soured and messes for which I was responsible did absolutely no good. After hitting rock bottom in that crummy apartment in South Atlanta, I spent time digging deep and figuring out what I needed to apologize for and what I needed to let go of if making amends wasn't received or possible. I decided to treat my life as if I was preparing for the most important inspections of my military career. I wanted to not only pass but have the shiniest boots, the cleanest uniform, and the neatest quarters. That required the same kind of attention to detail and dedication to excellence that got me named Soldier of the Year for my battalion.

Besides, after two assignments serving as an Inspector General, I'd spent years listening to the problems of others and helping find resolution. Moreover, I knew how messy things could get if I tried to hide from them. **Any good soldier knows that in battle your problems can quickly multiply and become insurmountable. Anyone who has raised their hand to defend their nation knows that war can bring casualties and situations we did not expect to happen.**

Ironically, even the bravest soldier in battle may run from conflict on the home front. We put on our armor and guard our hearts, emotions, and egos as if our lives depend on being impenetrable. It seems counterintuitive, but the strongest among us are the ones willing to make themselves vulnerable with family and friends. To clear your decks with others and deal with issues that have been created or are lingering, you must ask for help, forgiveness, and grace. Let's face it: all of us have plenty of issues both from our pasts and from transition. Only when we acknowledge that fact and address them one by one can we move forward.

When I speak of resolving issues, I'm really speaking about

two things. One is resolving conflicts with people; the other is resolving issues within yourself that cause anxiety, discomfort, anger, or depression.

Johnny Birch

Enlisted in 1999 out of high school. Part of demonstration team in Korea. Had bricks broken on head, which resulted in a mild TBI. Also had PTSD, depression. Supposed to be promoted but passed over due to injury. Medically discharged in 2005, thirty days from being deployed to Afghanistan.

The hard part was not knowing where I would end up. I lost our house and had to file bankruptcy, and almost lost my family. I work at a school for special education—behavior problems, learning disabilities—teaching taekwondo. Training for staff started in late August, but the Army would not release me. Luckily a group of people contacted the military for me so I wouldn't lose the job, which was a blessing. I don't know what would have happened if that issue had not been resolved. I worked there for ten years and now run my own taekwondo school.

When you look at the list of top stressors in life—moving, job loss, death of a loved one, and many others—military personnel, veterans, and our families score off the charts. We have work conflicts brought on by the incredible stress of the demands of service to our country: living with orders from someone else, danger we cannot control, moving around at a moment's notice, constantly working with new groups of people, and dealing with the subsequent relationship conflicts. Military spouses and family have to deal with everything military personnel deal with at some level, plus their own loads of issues brought on by shouldering the burdens of inadequate income, constant moves, and the absence (and then return) of a loved one who expects to drop back into their lives.

Conflict is natural and inevitable but not inherently bad. The problem can affect our ability to be productive or caring or even to making a living. Or maybe the issue can be seen as an opportunity for learning and growth. In either case, we need to work toward a resolution. When we resolve issues, we strengthen ourselves, our relationships, and may bring some peace into the world around us.

Deciding on strategies for resolving issues depends on what the issue is. Because there is nothing military personnel love more than having a strategy, you probably already have the skill set to deal with your issues. After all, the military is all about conflict resolution. You just need to shift your thinking. Can your issue be a win-win collaboration? Or do you see it a win-lose situation where your win will be confrontational and perhaps contested? Because I can tell you right now, you don't really walk away from win-lose issues. They tend to perpetuate more issues that need to be resolved.

Remember: if one person leaves a conflict feeling wounded, the conflict is not over.

Until you start to take responsibility for your part in a conflict, you can't hope to resolve any real issues, even if you think you won. **You have to face your problems and reach out to repair damaged relationships or suffer the consequences, which I guarantee will hold you back.**

Resolving financial issues is a sticky issue for couples in the service. I struggled quite a bit financially during my time in the Army, especially in the early years. I even had to declare bankruptcy at one point. Denise, my third—and lifelong—wife knew this when she married me. Luckily, she persevered and got her nursing degree and most recently became a nurse practitioner. I was able to go from below poverty-level income with child support payments in my previous life to having a master's degree and law degree and being in a zone of comfort with a home in Hawaii.

After I retired, getting my retirement pay and disability pay required a tremendous amount of patience and perseverance due to a bureaucratic snafu. Despite my request that my pay go into the same account it always had, the government inexplicably sent it to a nonexistent USAA account. Of course, that bureaucratic nightmare caused a lot of conflict with my wife, who was understandably upset when it took more than six months to get it rectified and put us in a position where we had to take out a bank loan to pay our bills. I spent hours on the phone, requested help from my congressman, took names and dates down, and still hit roadblock after roadblock. But I kept hammering away until I finally got what was due to me.

I share that to illustrate that **even when you think you've secured your position, you can still find that you come under an unexpected, unprovoked, and prolonged attack.**

The important thing is to work together on the problem and not to give up on one another. As a couple, we dug into our foxhole and became battle buddies. When the love started getting deeper, the income started going up, and along with it, our emotional connection started getting richer.

We lived out of boxes for fourteen years. Nobody likes to live like that. But we became more resilient as we began figuring out how to solve problems together. We found ways to save. We bought some real estate and sold it, making a little bit of money with that. We took turns improving our opportunities by increasing our education.

Because we kept at it and had small goals and larger goals, I can now focus on the things that I am passionate about—and that is speaking to you and sharing *Warrior's Code 001* and the 7 Vital Steps to Resiliency, which have transformed my life and that of my family. I've pledged to faithfully serve my fellow veterans and their families for the remainder of my life because of my gratitude for what I've learned. My wife and family support my new mission.

A wonderful book by a successful conflict-resolution mediation consultant is *Peace in Everyday Relationships: Resolving Conflicts in Your Personal and Work Life*. Sheila Alson and Gayle Burnett have drawn on the fields of neurology, psychology, teambuilding, communication skills, negotiation, martial arts, alternative dispute resolution, law, education, diversity, training, and spirituality to find workable solutions to our very human issues.

The first part is titled ever so aptly, "Changing the Way We Fight." To do this, let's also consider a term proposed by Daniel Goleman in his book *Emotional Intelligence: Why It Can Matter More Than IQ*: "emotional hijacking" is a response to our physiological fight-or-flight warning system. It seems our brains are still wired the way they were three hundred years ago—for a quick response to danger. This is oh so important in many military situations, but in civilian life, it is why the counter-warning "count to ten" was invented. We have about an eight-second delay before our intellect catches up with our emotion. During that time, we've got adrenaline pumping to energize our muscles, increased heart rate and rapid breathing to get oxygen to the blood to carry to our extremities, dilated pupils and tunnel vision to enhance our sight.

If we do not take time for our brain to respond instead of our body, we will give in to either aggression/fight to protect ourselves, even though the situation may not actually be dangerous, or fearfulness/flight, leaving the situation as quickly as possible, also for our protection. This is called emotional hijacking, which is a shortcut to saying the brain's amygdala is holding the neocortex hostage.

The antidote to this fight or flight, which causes so many issues in our lives, is to understand what is happening and to practice a "counterattack," to slow down our automatic response. PAUSE. Do count to ten if you can. Then COOL DOWN. Breathe deeply instead of shallowly. Blink. And drink some water before responding if at all possible. I can tell you right now that the more people I spoke with regarding the stall of my pay, the angrier I got. I had to practice these principles to keep from losing my mind.

When I first started working with my coauthor, Echo Garrett, on this project, she could tell that my default was to get angry about past situations. She gave me a book called *Battlefield of the Mind: Winning the Battle in Your Mind* by Joyce Meyer. By the time I finished reading it, there was hardly a page without at least one sticky note. Ironically, Meyer grew up close to where I did in Missouri. She describes all the ways our minds get attacked by self-condemnations, depression, and more.

This battle is winnable, but it takes tremendous effort and being cognizant of your triggers. One of mine is feeling disrespected, because I grew up with so much criticism and being told I'd never be anything. What are the triggers that set you off?

BRETT HALE

My biggest battle was when I returned home from Afghanistan and retired from the Army. Being 100 percent disabled, I was no longer able to work in the pharmaceutical sales profession I had been in before. There were so many issues to resolve. The Wounded Warrior Project has been a godsend for me on multiple occasions, setting up counseling for me, for instance. My next biggest battle after my health was divorce and a civil lawsuit filed against my ex and her parents for significant invasion of privacy. I spent $150,000 in legal bills. The first eighteen months of the suit I did not see my three kids, but now I have a great relationship with them.

During a conflict, observe yourself. Is this who you are? Touch base with your cognitive self. What are you thinking now that you are no longer in an emotional whirlwind? Can you respond from your heart instead of your emotions or intellect? If so, do so. Practice this over and over every time you are in a situation that challenges your emotions but is non-life-threatening. And give yourself a pat on the back because it is not easy to tame your fight-or-flight response.

Alson and Burnett point out that there is a conflict cycle, which consists of cause, incident, response, and outcome. I would hope the outcome would be resolution.

The cause is usually pretty easy to identify: an economic conflict/not enough money, a value conflict/conflicting beliefs, a power conflict/one person or entity asserting more influence over the other. The incident is made up of details that are just various scenarios that most likely fall under these categories.

To make sure you understand the cause, however, break it down into smaller pieces. A given for quick resolution is that you stay in the present. But sometimes issues are more about the past. Is this a conflict that has escalated due to past unresolved issues? Do you or the other person carry around a "list of atrocities"? Are there other people involved in the conflict? Could this conflict be a cultural difference?

The response is where we get into trouble.

We have the fight-or-flight response of aggression or avoidance. Aggressive behavior, excluding physical violence, includes shouting, interrupting, threatening and ultimatums, insisting you are right, persistently trying to prove your point, nagging, revenge, and hurling insults. Avoidance behavior includes withdrawing physically, talking behind the other person's back, not talking, getting depressed or sick, acting super polite, using distractions to ignore the issue, telling yourself it doesn't matter or taking on the role of being a martyr, and taking it out on someone else.

None of those behaviors sounds promising. But there is an alternative: assertiveness. You can do this:

- Use an opening statement creating a "we" perspective to solving the issue, as in "We have a common interest here in solving this."
- Be an active listener, checking to make sure you have heard things correctly.
- Identify the other person's needs and feelings and state your own.
- Reduce defensiveness by using "I" statements instead of "You" statements, which is verbal finger-pointing.
- Reframe the situation in less negative terms, positively if you can.
- Brainstorm to look for win-win solutions. The outcome with being assertive is either resolution or agreeing to disagree.

One model of resolving issues that is rarely successful, and is actually a bad idea, is to assign blame. This action doesn't work in win-win negotiations, yet we hold on to it because judging people and assigning blame is probably something we were very good at in the past. The only time this action may help resolve a conflict is if you can blame an entity, like the legal system, or politicians as a whole. Getting blame off your chest and onto a generalized target can give you a respite as far as your responsibility for something that is truly out of your control. But if you don't let go of the emotions that go with blame, you are sitting in the same frying pan, turning over your complaints past the point of them being crispy. Frankly, no one is going to want to hear about it.

One thing that is so, so important in this step is to never give up. I guarantee you that anyone whose life you admire has doggedly persevered to resolve problems in their lives. Solutions, particularly like long-simmering family feuds, may not happen overnight, and it might be a bit messy for a while, but once you have worked this step, the spirit of it will allow you to resolve things you never thought could be settled.

Once you've become a peace negotiator and successfully navigated the emotional land mines of resolving an issue, you make a contribution to creating an environment of peace, where conflicts don't arise so often.

STEP 6

RECON TO MAP OUT YOUR FUTURE

Part of any serious mission in the military is doing recon to scope out strategic information. In wartime, "no-man's-land" exists between two enemy trench systems. But what really defines the territory of no-man's-land is fear. Neither side wishes to advance for fear of being attacked by the enemy in the process, which can create paralysis and panic. You never want to be no-man's-land, which is why you do recon.

This principle holds true as a civilian. Part of transition, which is one of the most serious missions in the rest of your life, is surveying the possibilities for your future. Now, instead of patrolling on foot, by ship or submarine, aircraft, satellite, or from covert observation posts, you need to scout out and prepare for transitioning by zeroing in on the logistics of your new mission in life.

PERRY WEST

Joined Navy. Father was career Air Force. Primarily worked as nuclear weapons missile technician. First-Class Petty Officer E-6.

When you are in the military, you don't have to think about certain things in your life. They are taken care of for you and you don't even know it. When you get out, there is not a lot of direction about what life is going to be like. I had never lived in the DC area before. I had difficulty getting a job and was unemployed for the first six months. Also, I did not realize the job market would be flooded. After I got a job, it was shocking how I could barely live on what I was making. Between that and child support, I was working sixty hours of overtime a week and barely making ends meet. I wish I'd been better prepared for those first few years out of the service. Today I work for Oracle as a senior support engineer.

Do not wait until you are a civilian to do your recon. One of the biggest mistakes veterans make is they don't have a plan. When the military has taken care of you for a decade or more, you forget how much things cost off of the base and how expensive civilian-life housing is. Suddenly you have to think about all these additional bills that had been covered. Then things in every other area of your life start showing up undone.

You usually know eighteen months in advance when you will be leaving the military. It seems like a slow process, but you'll need every bit of that time and more for planning. Sometimes you can start taking education courses before you are out of the service. All of us should take advantage of the GI Bill benefits toward education.

Before you venture into new territory, take into account your status in regard to finances, health, education, vocation, and relationships: where you are and where you want to be. Let yourself dream big and explore your most ambitious hopes. Create a vision map that shows your priorities. Examine your goals, align them with your priorities, and create a detailed action plan that will get you headed in the right direction.

Ask for help if you need it, and you probably will because paperwork is one of the most frustrating problems you will face immediately. You are going to need a résumé, for instance, but military skills don't always translate to civilian life. They should, but military responsibilities and titles are often ignored in the outside world, which does not take the time to understand the jargon. Meanwhile, just filling out discharge papers and routing payments to your bank can become a monumental task when you are faced with institutionalized bureaucracy. Remember that in my case my payments somehow went to a different Mark Green, and it took six months of persistence to fix that flaw.

Any pilot knows that a flight plan always needs adjustments along the way. Expect that your plan needs to be flexible, too. You are worth the time investment it takes to develop a good plan fleshed out with a smart strategy, concrete goals, and a map to get you where you want to go.

On May 13, 2000, I began journaling with the idea of putting down my goals in every area of my life: personal, professional, and financial goals. I started dreaming about what I wanted my future to look like. I found myself adding areas to my journal that made up a complete personal-development strategy. It was my way of reconnecting with myself over and over as I wrote down and read my goals and strategy for attaining them. More than three years prior to what ended up being my actual retirement date, I began planning for it.

I was uncertain, so I pursued a two-prong course of action. On one hand, I behaved as if I were going for the next promotion, but I also made contact with resources that would help me start my own business in case I wanted to do that.

As I completed goals, I marked a line through them with a thick red marker. I kept up this process, refining it in subsequent journals to reflect more clarity, adding quotes and affirmations, and creating a full mission statement for my life, envisioning every area of my life with the steps and tasks in front of me. In my memoir, *Step Out, Step Up,* I chronicled the impact goals have had on my life. Without them, you are simply treading water. Life is a game of goals within goals and every objective is completed incrementally.

The book *See You at the Top* by Zig Ziglar, first published in 1975, gave me ideas and motivation when my passion was held hostage by life events sometimes too unbearable to relive. Ziglar calls *See You at the Top* the "how-to" book that gives you a "check-up" from the "neck up," to eliminate "stinkin' thinkin'" and avoid "hardening of the attitudes."

Jaclyn Peters

I left the military at a later date than I originally wanted to because I realized I did not have a good enough plan for my future. I had watched friends struggle when they got out, and I didn't want to go through that by myself. One of my duties as a Marine was to be a part of funeral honors for one of the Marines who had been part of our unit, who was killed in an accident shortly after we returned to the States. You do twelve-hour watches over the casket at the funeral home, and the fallen soldier is never left alone. I had a rapport with the grieving family. I also got to tour the prep room at the funeral home and talk to the employees. I researched mortuary schools and started online courses. I was about halfway through when I got out of the military. When there was a full-time opening at the Franklin County Coroner's Office in Columbus, Ohio, I became a forensic technician, investigating and collecting evidence regarding the cause of death besides checking out the body.

As you begin your reconnaissance and planning, look inward first. What do you enjoy doing? How can you make a living doing it? Why do you love doing that particular thing? Dig deeper. What is your big WHY? If you didn't believe failure was even a possibility, if you acted fearlessly, what would be your ultimate dream?

What makes you truly and abundantly happy? For some

people, it's being able to provide for their family. For others, it's giving back to their community. Some people like to travel, explore, learn, create and build, or mentor—whatever it is that drives you, put yourself in position to be plugged into your source of joy to remain energized and stay in the fight. If your passion aligns with your dream, you will always have fuel in the tank to keep moving forward.

In my case, I knew that I wanted to be a resiliency and transition coach after completing thirty-four years of service, but I did not wait until year thirty-four to begin executing my plan. I started three years prior to my retirement in the fall of 2017. I knew this next stage of life would start with people and expanding my network. Just like in warfare, you must have allies. The self-made person is a myth. Nobody accomplishes anything great 100 percent alone.

One of the networking strategies I applied that helped me grow my own network out rapidly was to write down a list of ten people I could sit down and share my dream with. Don't ask for a job. Instead, ask for a couple of other people who might be useful to speak with or send a résumé to. This technique multiplied my connections and ensured my network was value driven. Absorb as much information from these conversations; that way you never leave an opportunity empty-handed—knowledge is more precious than gold. Make it clear up front you are not asking for a job to remove a sense of obligation and pressure. That's the way 90 percent of people get jobs and crack open new opportunities for themselves.

Next, I threw myself headfirst into intensive public-speaking training to learn how to motivate, inspire, instill vision, and share *Warrior's Code 001* and the curriculum derived from the 7 Vital Steps to Resiliency with the world. Great leaders lead by example and are constantly looking for new ways to grow. I identified a weakness and sought to not only eliminate it, but to master it.

I also went through several programs for "vetrepreneurs" and also connected with the University of Central Florida in Orlando, which offers many resources for veterans. I used the Army Corporate Partners Program, Boots to Business, started attended meetings with the Mayor's Veteran Council, and became a Success Principles–trained coach to prepare for the future. Each of these connections helped me uncover and change limiting beliefs, create focus and clarity and a path to success for my company.

What I realized along the way is that I was improving myself so I could improve others. There are forty thousand programs to help veterans in this country, but you have to do the digging yourself and ask for what you want. In one program, the military matches you up with a mentor. That program led me to Lisa Sharkey, previously senior producer of *Good Morning America* and now senior vice president of creative development at HarperCollins Publishers. What she taught me was to listen to those who have done it. She shared vital tips on how to structure my first book and gave me direction. I listened. She suggested I become a certified trainer.

What I have learned to do is look at what you want to be and what you want to do and surround yourself with those already doing it. Listen to smart, talented people.

Recon should be pleasurable and satisfying if you start on it early. It's such a great opportunity to get to know yourself, whether you are an officer or enlistee. What do you want to do with the next stage of your life? **This is the time to go for it, determine your purpose, and accept your next mission as a warrior.**

STEP 7

REENGAGE AND GET ON WITH IT!

One of the best ways to reengage is to continue to be of service in some way. You probably went into the military to serve your country. No matter what your passion or path will be, giving back and supporting others adds purpose and meaning to life.

If you are already practicing the first six Rs of resilience, you have some gas in your tank. You can still be the first line of defense against bad people and threats to peace, with one important shift. In the military, you may have had to harden your heart to follow orders and perform your duties. This is the time to soften your heart.

Tim Boone

When I was in the military, I was fortunate to be stationed at Fort Ord in Monterey, California, where I got into leadership training and met psychologists and social workers who believed in me. That later turned into a forty-five-year career for me.

Currently, I am the volunteer chair of the board of advisors for Warrior2Citizen (https://www.warrior2citizen.org/), *an organiza-*

tion built by warriors for warriors. We focus on troops and their families during that critical period when they return home from war zones. W2C programs are designed to provide high-quality, focused psychological and spiritual counseling for the warrior and their family in a peaceful setting that will nurture the healing process without outside distractions. Returning veterans have unique transition issues that include moral injury, relocating, finding employment, readjusting to family life, recreating their identity from soldier to civilian, and reestablishing many other relationships. It's a very intense program and gets vets to take risks with their spouses quickly and be really vulnerable and honest with each other. They learn what it means to be best friends and to have a safe haven where everyone knows the difficulties they are facing. We help them find the motivation to move on and regenerate, and teach them if you see a buddy suffering, reach out and help them.

You already have an air of authority from your time in the military, no matter your rank. You've been well trained and people notice that: your posture, your direct and polite form of address, hopefully your confidence. The tone of the country today is to honor our veterans for their service. This means most folks respect you right out of the gate. If you approach potential employers, new neighbors, or your fellow students in courses with a positive attitude, it will most likely come right back at you. It has been shown that the more you show people you care, the more people listen to you, gravitate to you, and appreciate you. You will be making friends before you know it.

Friends are your ticket to both professional and social networking, which will speed your reengagement in civilian life.

It is also important to reengage with old friends. In the military we tend to be casual about keeping up friendships because we move around so much. One of the best things I did in my transition was to reconnect with my taekwondo buddies. Besides renewing my passion for this martial art, I felt so much gratitude and appreciation for these two men, Rafael Medina and Pedro Laboy, who had been on a journey with me to push ourselves to be agile, focused, and fast. It also helped me to reengage with taekwondo itself, which requires concentration, equilibrium, breath control, power, and speed—physical skills that transfer to the mind and spirit.

Now I am totally embedded in the veterans' community in Orlando. The University of Central Florida, which has the largest veteran student population in the country, is very active in a program that shares veterans' stories, documenting them, through the Veterans History Project made possible by the generous support of the United States Congress that was created in 2002. Our personal stories are powerful. It's important to share them so more people can understand what it is to serve your country and be a veteran. Ninety-eight percent of the population has no frame of reference for our experiences.

Greg Pace

Attended US Naval Academy in Annapolis. Commissioned as a Second Lieutenant in US Marine Corps. Captain and Executive Officer of Alpha Company, Headquarters Battalion, Marine Corps in Arlington, Virginia. Left service in 1993. Currently national director, Military and Veterans Affairs, DeVry University, San Diego.

Giving back to the brother- and sisterhood of individuals who have served is more rewarding than any job I have ever had. I have the experience and knowledge to help them avoid the pitfalls and navigate transition to civilian life. Civilians recognize the level of experience of a General or Colonel. They can build up their own network and more readily find opportunities. But mid- to lower-rank enlisted men and women don't have the same level of education and network for hiring managers to recognize them as valuable. Veterans need to get their training and education and then understand how to market and brand themselves. Military jargon and acronyms are impactful for them, but not for a civilian manager.

One caution I want to put out there. Your job in this step is to fully reengage, not partially reengage. When we've been away from our families and friends, we got used to Facebooking, FaceTiming, texting, and emailing. Screen time and digital messaging do not provide true emotional contact. Make plans to actually meet with people, shake their hand, look them in the eye. There is a depth of engagement that comes from face-to-face interaction that cannot be approximated.

Reengaging applies to your routine activities and special commitments as well. Be present for whatever you are doing. Give yourself over to the task at hand mindfully, not mindlessly. You may have gotten used to performing expected duties automatically. When you are living with others, sharing chores and helping each other, you need to bring your whole self, not just your body.

That said, as you reengage with family and friends, know your purpose and set boundaries. Respect others' boundaries as well. Many of us want to drop back into our old life, which is impossible because our old life adapted to our absence and moved on without us. At the same time, nonmilitary family and friends may not realize you need quiet time to process the changes you have been going through. Ask yourself what matters most at any given moment and make that your priority.

Mentally resilient people bounce back and move on. With all the proactive steps you've taken toward the next stage in your life, you stand a much better chance of creating a positive, balanced life centered on your priorities and values. In order for me to reengage, I decided to create a big idea, a clear message, and find an army of advocates to further my cause. You are one of those advocates. I need your stories, your commitment to be your best and never give up on yourself. I like the African proverb "If you want to go fast, go alone. If you want to go far, go together." We are a community of unity with the Warrior's Code. There is a secret message in this book. See if you can find it. If you do, it means you read it and now you see it.

Congratulations on working through the 7 Steps with your family and friends, on your well-being and attitude, on your future and your purpose, your dreams, and most importantly, yourself. You are back in the fight in every area of your life. Ready to move forward? Permission granted.

YOUR PLEDGE TO YOURSELF

With transition, there is no one size fits all. We are all unique individuals, and our situations are all different. By getting the basics of 7 Vital Steps to Resiliency embedded in our core, we find our true self. As you navigate this information, understand that more than one of these steps can be happening at the same time. We call that life. We can draw strength from finding new ways to look at our situations not only from our own perspectives, but also from input and communication with others. Everything starts with your willingness to try. Even if we fail the first time we try to move forward—or the first dozen times—keep trying. Keep moving forward by applying the 7 Steps to any area—finances, relationships, work, mental or physical health—you know you need to work on.

Bouncing back from physical, mental, and spiritual trauma is difficult. Our timelines might be different, and those *aha* moments when we learn of a new tool or habit that helps us become a better person may take longer than you like. In my first book, I warned that in order to move forward we may need to lose a little ego. This can be a true test to some, as we have achieved some amazing things while in the military and may not be willing to let go of our old selves and identities as we attempt to assimilate into the civilian world.

Our old behaviors and the battle mindset may have served us well in the past and even kept us alive. But we are going new places that require different behaviors and a shift in mindset. If you follow this program and commit to the basics of the Warrior's Code, you will have friends, resources, experience, and wisdom on your side. You'll identify your purpose.

I personally have conquered many challenges of mind, body, and spirit during the years leading up to and continuing into my own transition. I shared the valuable lessons I learned through trial and error in this book and my memoir, *Step Out, Step Up*. Now it's your time to navigate your own obstacle course during the basic training of *Warrior's Code 001* on your way to writing your new story and creating your future. Step out of a defeatist mindset and step up to positive thinking. Use your subconscious mind to build better resilience. Your journey toward triumphant transition can be the best time of your life once you set your mind to making the Warrior's Code work for you, your family, and others. Work on you and watch the magic of better resilience make any change easier. I believe you can. Now you must believe in yourself.

Please answer the questions in the next section with honesty, and for those that require a number, circle the number that fits you best in this pre-resilience contract with yourself, so you can later take a post-transition questionnaire to identify if you have increased your resilience. Please visit my website at www.mark.green to complete the digital contract and questions along with a few basic identifying questions, all of which will be kept confidential. However, if you want to share your story in order to help others or possibly participate in Warrior's Code workshops in the future, please indicate that so you can be considered for inclusion in future Warrior's Code media and events. Once you provide your email and both your pre-results from when you started reading the book and your post-results after implementing the 7 Vital Steps to Resiliency, you will receive a Certificate of Resilience from Warrior's Code 001. We use these answers to help guide our evidence-based Warrior's Code 001 curriculum, and your responses will remain anonymous.

WARRIOR'S CODE CONTRACT AND QUESTIONS

Step 1: REST to Be Your Best

I will rest in a way that rejuvenates me physically and mentally. This is "my time" for resting and strengthening my mind, body, and spirit so I can rebuild my life and regenerate my commitment. I agree to slow down enough so that it makes a difference for me, and those around me and my family and friends agree to work with me to allow that time. These times may not always be at the same time of the day, and rest can include other things that are not just for the mind, body, and spirit. It can include a vacation or time on my own or with family and friends; it can include a retreat to the outdoors or other restful activities. **Caution: take the time you need, but do not get complacent.** It is not okay to rest on your heels indefinitely.

What do you do to rest now?

What are **three things** you would like to do to rest?

What could you do **right now** that you are not doing that would make a difference today?

On a scale of one to ten with ten being **fully rested**, what number on the scale would you pick right now?

| 1 | 2 | 3 | 4 | 5 | 6 | 7 | 8 | 9 | 10 |

Step 2: RECONNECT with Yourself and Others

Anytime I am away and return from training deployments or long trips, I agree to take time to reconnect with myself and family or friends. I will do this in many different ways: by writing letters, hanging out with GOOD friends, spending quality time with myself or others, and communicating things that are important to me and allowing others to do the same with the things that are important to them. There is no definite timeline on this. I will work toward positive social and personal interaction regularly. Absence changes us. See it for what it is. It may be hard for everyone, not just you. I promise it is okay to remind me of my commitment during reconnection without fearing I will treat others poorly for doing so. **Caution: reconnecting with harmful things, harmful habits, or harmful friends or family is not part of this picture.** Your goal is to reconnect in healthy ways with beneficial activities and with people who are important to you now or whom you feel you want to know better because they would be good mentors or role models. Set strong boundaries and do not wander off into any emotional war zones.

What can you do to **open up** and talk about how you feel as you return?

What **activities** beyond intimacy can you do to reconnect with those you are with every day, including family and friends?

What would be something you can do right now to **increase communication** after returning from time away?

On a scale of one to ten with ten being **fully reconnected**, what number on the scale would you pick right now?

| 1 | 2 | 3 | 4 | 5 | 6 | 7 | 8 | 9 | 10 |

Step 3: RESET Your Mind

I will take time to work on my mindset. This is fundamentally one of the most important steps. My attitude and the attitudes of others can bring triumphant transition or destroy it. I will use all available means to support and supplement my plan for remarkable resilience. That can include through reading, social media, friends, family, clergy, and other qualified specialists in all areas of life to keep a strong mindset during transitions. I will communicate to others that the use of personal space may be required at times so I can practice calm, thoughtful responses, and all agree to give me that space to do so. If I ever feel that I am at a point that

I cannot continue or handle things, I agree to tell someone I need help to work on things I do not understand. If I ever feel like I would hurt myself or others, I will stop, share that immediately, and work with professionals and those closest to me to get the help I need. I understand that the people in my life deserve to continue to enjoy and celebrate life, as I do. Time heals, and there are thousands of people and organizations available to help me reset. I know I must not isolate myself, and I commit to creating habits and changes that will bring me to a proper and positive mindset, positioned for positive change.

Do you **meditate**, and would you try it if it helps calm the mind?

Do you **exercise**, and if not, would you start?

Do you want to **build mind, body, and spirit** to make great choices going forward?

Do you have **written affirmations, quotes, and morning routines** that help you prepare for your day?

On a scale of one to ten with ten being the highest, what number on the scale would you pick right now on **how strong is your mind**?

| 1 | 2 | 3 | 4 | 5 | 6 | 7 | 8 | 9 | 10 |

On a scale of one to ten with ten being the highest, what number on the scale would you pick right now on **how strong is your body**?

| 1 | 2 | 3 | 4 | 5 | 6 | 7 | 8 | 9 | 10 |

On a scale of one to ten with ten being the highest, what number on the scale would you pick right now on **how strong is your spirit**?

| 1 | 2 | 3 | 4 | 5 | 6 | 7 | 8 | 9 | 10 |

Step 4: REMOVE Negativity

I will identify problems with negativity and write them down along with options of what would help me deal with them. I will come up with contingencies if the first solution does not work. I will take action to remove negative emotions and negative people and to ban "stinkin' thinkin'." Letting go of negativity is extremely important in moving toward living out the Warrior's Code. I don't just let go of negative things; I replace them with positive ones. I will identify my triggers for negative emotions and enlist those closest to me to help me avoid them. I will ask for help, with no shame, when I am stuck in negativity. I will replace negative thoughts with kind thoughts. When all else fails, I will laugh. And always, every day, I will have an attitude of gratitude.

Have you surrounded yourself with positive people who create a positive environment?

Are you reaching out to people with kindness and compassion? Do you ask for help when you need it?

Do you keep a gratitude journal, and what kinds of things do you write in it? I suggest writing at least three things in your journal for which you are grateful on a daily basis. Read over them often to boost your spirits.

How grateful are you at this moment?

| 1 | 2 | 3 | 4 | 5 | 6 | 7 | 8 | 9 | 10 |

Step 5: RESOLVE Issues

I will resolve and deal with larger issues by coming up with a plan that chunks it down into steps and tasks. I will create a timeline with specific actions, and if any of those actions do not turn out as I planned, I will adjust and keep focused on the end state. I will not quit. I will keep moving forward to resolve large and small issues in my life. These may be personal, professional, health, or finance related. I will write them down and envision what I see happening to fix them. I also know that if I fail, I will fail forward and also search out others who may be experts at resolving my issues.

Do you have lots of **unresolved issues** right now? If so, will you write them down here, or in a notebook, right now?

Have you already worked with others on these issues? How many have been resolved, and what do you still need to work on?

When you think about how many major issues you need to resolve, where do you rank yourself?

| 1 | 2 | 3 | 4 | 5 | 6 | 7 | 8 | 9 | 10 |

Step 6: RECON to Map Out Your Future

I understand my future is up to me. I have already or will set goals—not just in my head. I will write them down and set timelines with a specific date and time of the day that I will complete them by. I will revisit them often, and if a major life event happens that affects my ability to not reach it, I promise to readjust the goal or remove it if necessary. I agree to break down my goals into the steps I will take, and then on top of that identify the tasks I must take under each step. I understand I am not a failure if I do not reach a goal and that it is okay to push it to the right if necessary. Life happens, and everyone helping me achieve my goals understands that. My written goals must meet the criteria for a good goal. I realize that without action after I write them, nothing happens. I MUST take action! I have a journal where I have collected my goals in every important area of my life: personal, professional, fitness, faith, family, and any other area important to me. I will write affirmations to reach my goals and visualize the feeling I get when I achieve them. I will add new goals as new opportunities become available.

Have you written out goals using the process discussed above?

Have you reached any of your goals or added new ones?

Will you build a goal plan timeline and use affirmations to already see yourself achieving them?

On a scale of one to ten with ten being the highest, what number on the scale would you pick right now if you scored yourself on the presence of **written goals**?

| 1 | 2 | 3 | 4 | 5 | 6 | 7 | 8 | 9 | 10 |

Step 7: REENGAGE and Get On with It!

I am ready to reengage and truly live my life with love and joy no matter the past circumstances or events. It is not the events in my life that define my future, it is my response to them that equals the outcome. *The Success Principles* is one of the books I will reference for future growth as I reengage. It will help me in many other areas of my life as well. I will express to others when I am ready to try to reengage physically or mentally. If I need help getting out of my comfort zone, I will face my fears and use the warrior spirt I already have in me. I know how to bring warrior intensity already and can see how those values will help me transition triumphantly. I know that living the Warrior's Code and taking the 7 Vital Steps to Resiliency will be an ongoing commitment. The rest of my life will be much different now. I embrace these changes and know that I will learn to love myself for who I am, where I am, and who I am with regardless of previous situations. I am resilient. I also agree to share my newfound tools and attitudes with others. This does not mean I have to let go of my tough-guy or tough-girl persona. It just means I am ready to engage life with a different mindset—one that will serve me and others.

Are you more prepared for transition after reading this *Warrior's CODE 001*?

On a scale of one to ten with ten being the highest, what number on the scale would you pick right now on **how resilient you are**?

| 1 | 2 | 3 | 4 | 5 | 6 | 7 | 8 | 9 | 10 |

By signing this page, I agree to work on my transition in a way that will help me and those around me see the value of being a living embodiment of the Warrior's Code in mind, body, and spirit. I pledge to apply the 7 Vital Steps to Resiliency to every aspect of my life and revisit them as often as necessary in order to keep my commitment to the Warrior's Code way.

Signature

____

LOOKING BACK AND LOOKING FORWARD

I have lost, and I have won. I am still competitive, but now I look for win-win collaborative solutions rather than win-lose confrontational solutions.

I am a survivor, not a victim. I no longer feel sorry for myself. When things go wrong, it is not because the deck is stacked against me. It is because I had choices, and I either did not take them or I made the wrong choice.

I was angry with the world. Now I find joy and gratitude in every area of my life.

I have achieved much on my own. But what is most important to me is the connections I have made with others.

I wanted material evidence of my success. I have learned that it is doing what you love that makes you a success.

I have learned that life is not always fair—and that everyone has problems. I am not unique in having to struggle. I am in good company.

My hardships did not beat me. They made me strong. My past led me to the present, where I am making plans for an amazing future.

I can control my attitude every day and make sure it is fresh, with no dirt on it from the day before. I recognize and accept that if I have a bad day, it is okay. Just readjust and let those kinds of moments pass. Off course or on course, constant correction is a fact of life.

When you come at life with love and joy, the real magic happens. Take the time to work on yourself, and great things will grow from the seeds you plant and from steps you take.

The journey of transition for me did not start when I left military service. It began when I started writing this book and I faced my old self. I was wearing a mask of ego that clouded out any strong emotional connection with others. I was putting way too much stock in my medals and fancy certificates and the stars, bars, and wreaths. I walked away from the possibility of promotion to full-bird Colonel in order to keep my promise to my wife and son that after years of moving, he could complete high school in one place and so I could tell my story to inspire others. More importantly, I want to hear your stories of transition and resilience—the good as well as your struggles and challenges.

I am on a quest to support you to draw on the same courage and persistence that got you through your service and bring it to civilian life.

I am not afraid to admit I needed some adjustments in my thinking and my life. There is strength in admitting our vulnerabilities. I found out that it was okay to step outside the old battle mindset and step up to the new.

It is not just talking to others that transformed me over these last three years. It was also the daily activities of resilience I practiced and the habits I began forming that altered my behavior:

The fact that I write out my affirmations on my mirror.

The fact that I have a meditation coach who walks me through guided meditation.

The fact that I can envision what I want my future to look like. Since I began doing that, many of the things I see in my mind are coming true.

The fact that I take the time to both exercise and rest when I need to.

I no longer cover up the compassion that I have inside. Instead of being judgmental, I have found myself wanting to go up to even those who have harmed me physically or emotionally and give them a hug.

It is easy to focus on the negative. Try being grateful for seven minutes every morning for everything you have for thirty days and see how it changes you.

Don't just look at how far you have to go. Think about how far you have come.

Transitioning to civilian life and integrating into your family unit, your friend circles, and your community is a journey, not a destination. Because you are never really finished with that journey, you must feel at home inside yourself.

I continue to have breakthroughs all the time in every area of my life. Our lives are like a suitcase. We put all our memories in them, but we have to choose what we're going to take out and wear. My days now after retirement of thirty-four years of Army service are spent telling the Army story and teaching others how to be resilient. Fight through the dark days. Push forward to be better and never, ever quit.

Follow good guidance from those who love you. Don't fight progress, invite it. Celebrate every new moment. Live life with all the intensity you can. Every second counts. You are here for a reason. Make that reason matter and understand that everything you do and everything you say affects others. Our tongues and words can become weapons too. Be present, be bold, be great, and do not worry what others think.

Remarkable resilience comes from committing to the Warrior's Code: taking responsibility, taking action, and getting rid of limiting beliefs, training our mindset and filling our minds with the right marching orders and positive content.

I am the Mindset Vet, and I strive to embody the change I want in others. Remember that you can find me easily online at www.mark.green, and I would not have written this book if you were not important. You matter, life matters, and the learning that takes place when we focus on ourselves can move mountains and millions of people. General Wesley Clark said, "It doesn't take any more energy to create a big dream than it does to create a little one." You deserve the best of everything after you have given of yourself to your country. They owe you that, but you cannot wait for it to show up at your door. I have given you the steps, now it is up to you to begin. Take the first step and the rest get easier.

I extend my deepest gratitude that you read this book. My

why is to build resilience in veterans and families because it will save lives and help get back to love and joy in our lives. My first big goal is to reach five hundred thousand veterans and first responders to learn the 7 Steps process. We are well on our way to reaching that goal.

Put one foot in front of the other. Accept the hand that reaches to pull you up and extend your hand to the next person. Go do great things. That's the spirit of a warrior—tried, tested, and true.

FROM THE AUTHORS

A special thanks to Melanie A. Bonvicino for pushing us to create this book, and to all the veterans and spouses who shared their stories with us. We honor your courage and thank you for being part of *Warrior's Code 001*.

BIBLIOGRAPHY

Alson, Sheila, and Gayle Burnett. *Peace in Everyday Relationships: Resolving Conflicts in Your Personal and Work Life*. Alameda, CA: Hunter House, 2003.

Amen, Daniel G. *Change Your Brain, Change Your Life*. New York: Three Rivers Press, 1999.

Army Surgeon General's Office. "Health of the Force." December 2015. www.armytimes.com/news/your-army/2015/12/13/army-report-shows-soldiers-lack-sleep-struggle-to-eat-right/.

Barker, Eric. "What the Music You Love Says About You and How It Can Improve Your Life." Time.com. March 10, 2014. http://time.com/16129/what-the-music-you-love-says-about-you-and-how-it-can-improve-your-life/.

Bergland, Christopher. "Your Brain Can Be Trained to Self-Regulate Negative Thinking." *Psychology Today*. January 10, 2016. https://www.psychologytoday.com/us/blog/the-athletes-way/201601/your-brain-can-be-trained-self-regulate-negative-thinking.

Goleman, Daniel. *Emotional Intelligence: Why It Can Matter More Than IQ*. New York: Bantam, 1996.

The American Institute of Stress. "The Holmes-Rahe Life Stresses Inventory." https://www.stress.org/holmes-rahe-stress-inventory/.

McNay, Shannon. "The High Cost of Sleep Deprivation." Military.com. http://www.military.com/benefits/veterans-health-care/the-high-cost-of-sleep-deprivation.html.

Meyer, Joyce. *Battlefield of the Mind: Winning the Battle in Your Mind*. New York: Warner Faith, 2002.

Millett, Maria. "Challenge Your Negative Thoughts." Michigan State University. March 31, 2017. http://msue.anr.msu.edu/news/challenge_your_negative_thoughts.

Sleep.Org. "Soldiers and Sleep: The Military's Shifting Stance." https://sleep.org/articles/military-sleep-issues/.

Staff report. "Study: Troops Don't Get Enough Sleep." *Military Times*. April 9, 2015. http://www.militarytimes.com/story/military/benefits/health-care/2015/04/09/study-says-servicemembers-not-sleeping-enough/25519353/.

Tan, Michelle. "Army Report Shows Soldiers Lack Sleep, Struggle to Eat Right." *Army Times*. December 13, 2015. https://www.armytimes.com/story/military/2015/12/13/army-report-shows-soldiers-lack-sleep-struggle-eat-right/77118466/.

Troxel, Wendy M., Regina A. Shih, Eric Pedersen, Lily Geyer, Michael P. Fisher, Beth Ann Griffin, Ann C. Haas, Jeremy R. Kurz, and Paul S. Steinberg. *Sleep in the Military: Promoting Healthy Sleep Among U.S. Servicemembers*. Santa Monica, CA: Rand Corporation, 2015.
http://www.rand.org/content/dam/rand/pubs/research_reports/RR700/RR739/RAND_RR739.pdf.

Winkle, Van. "Sleep Disorders among Troops More Damaging Than We Realize." *Task & Purpose*. April 25, 2016. http://taskandpurpose.com/sleep-disorders-among-troops-damaging-realize/.

Ziglar, Zig. *See You at the Top*. Gretna, LA: Pelican Publishing Company, 1975.

ABOUT THE AUTHORS

The Mindset Vet **Mark E. Green** started as a private in the US Army in December 1982 and retired as a Lieutenant Colonel on October 1, 2017, without a break in service, with twenty-four of his thirty-four years being active duty. He served as a paratrooper in the 82nd Airborne, where he was named Soldier of the Year for his battalion; served in the National Guard as a combat arms enlisted and officer; and served as an Army Reserve full-time soldier. He served in Afghanistan as an Inspector General in charge of the southern half of the country along the red desert from the borders of Pakistan to Iran. As a young soldier, he was also a founding member of the taekwondo team that went to the nationals and got the US Army to recognize it as an official sport.

Green has devoted the remainder of his career to helping those in military service, veterans, and their families with resiliency and transition. He holds a doctorate of law from Taft Law School, Santa Ana, California, and a master's degree in organizational management and communications from Concordia University, St. Paul, Minnesota. He is also a Jack Canfield–Certified Success Principles Coach; a graduate of Boots to Business program of Syracuse University; the Army Corporate

Partner (ACP) Mentorship Program, and SCORRE Speakers Training; and is a member of Lake Nona Toastmasters.

He developed the 7 Vital Steps to Resiliency from his own experiences in the military with his family, hard-earned lessons, and education, and is developing curriculum around them.

His company, My Silver Boots™, is a Florida-based, veteran-owned, made-in-the-USA small business, which has earmarked 10 percent of its profits to be divided among nonprofits that serve veterans and their families; underserved youth dealing with poverty, homelessness, or foster care; and US Army athletes. Green resides with wife, Denise, and teenage son Adam in Florida. As one of the nation's top experts on military transition, Green, who shares his life story in *Step Out, Step Up: Lessons Learned from a Lifetime of Transitions and Military Service*, thrives on speaking about resilience and transformational change.

Echo Montgomery Garrett is the coauthor of *Step Out, Step Up* in addition to *My Orange Duffel Bag: A Journey to Radical Change*, winner of the American Society of Journalists and Authors (ASJA) 2013 Arlene Eisenberg Award for Writing That Makes a Difference, which is only awarded every three years to a book that's made the biggest difference in people's lives. The book won six other national awards and two international awards for best book design, and it garnered Garrett the title of Georgia Author of the Year from the Georgia chapter of the National League of American Pen Women. She cofounded the Orange Duffel Bag Initiative (www.theodbi.org), an award-winning nonprofit that does life-plan coaching based on the principles in the book for homeless youth, high-poverty youth, and those aging out of foster care. She has written or contributed to fourteen other books, including *Why Don't They Just Get a Job?: One Couple's Mission to End Poverty in Their Community*. The Marietta, Georgia–based writer's work has been published in more than one hundred national media outlets, including *Parade, Delta Sky, Success*, and *The Atlanta Journal-Constitution*. She has been interviewed on *Good Morning America*, CNBC, CNN, and NY-1, and has served as editor in chief of *Atlanta Woman* magazine. Married to professional photographer Kevin Garrett, the couple resides in Marietta, Georgia, and has two adult sons, who are also entrepreneurs.